fro

ɔhould be returned or rene
ove

About the author

After leaving school, Benjamin Mee spent five years working in the building trade. Having taken a Psychology degree at University College London and an MSc in Science Communication at Imperial College London, he became a science and health journalist. He writes a DIY column for the *Guardian Weekend* magazine.

Acknowledgements

The author and publishers would like to thank the following for their help in the preparation of this book: Ian Davis, David Holloway, Dr Harriet Kimble, Mike Lawrence, Peter McCarthy, Patricia Newman, Allison Parkes, Janine Paterson, Michael Reynolds. The author would also like to thank numerous officials and press officers from a multitude of trade associations, professional bodies and government departments.

Getting the Best From Your Builder

Benjamin Mee

CONSUMERS' ASSOCIATION

Which? Books are commissioned by
Consumers' Association and published by
Which? Ltd, 2 Marylebone Road, London NW1 4DF
Email: books@which.net

Distributed by The Penguin Group:
Penguin Books Ltd, 80 Strand, London WC2R 0RL

First edition February 2004

Copyright © 2004 Which? Ltd

This book incorporates material from the Which? Book of Home Improvements by Mike
Lawrence

British Library Cataloguing in Publication Data
A catalogue record for Getting the Best from Your Builder is available from the British Library

ISBN 0 85202 928 4

For a full list of Which? books, please call 0800 252100, access our website at
www.which.net, or write to Which? Books, Freepost, PO Box 44, Hertford SG14 1SH.

Editorial and production: Joanna Bregosz, Ian Robinson, Mary Sunderland, Barbara Toft
Index: Marie Lorimer
Original cover concept by Sarah Harmer
Cover photograph by Peter Denton/getty images

Typeset by Saxon Graphics Ltd, Derby
Printed and bound in Great Britain by Creative Print and Design, Wales

Throughout this book for 'he' read 'he or she'

Contents

★An asterisk next to the name of an organisation in the text indicates that its address and/or contact details can be found in this section

Foreword

Why do builders have a bad name? Recent independent research carried out for the Federation of Master Builders (FMB) found that one in six homeowners has had a serious problem with their builder. But the research highlighted a common pattern. Those who experienced serious problems were the ones who had tended to get only a verbal estimate for the work. They were often looking to get it done on the cheap and frequently had not thought through what they wanted.

In contrast, those least likely to have experienced problems were the ones who had made sure they got written quotations, based on a detailed specification. They had selected their builder carefully, based on quality, value for money and proven expertise. They had checked out claims to membership of reputable trade bodies, such as the FMB, and they had protected themselves against disasters by insisting on insurance-backed guarantees for the work.

So, if you want to avoid your building job becoming a nightmare the message is clear. Do your homework first.

Most builders want to do a good job. A reputable professional builder will be happy to provide you with references so that you can check out his credentials before you take the plunge. A builder's dream customer is someone who knows what they want and is prepared to pay for it.

Having the builders in can be a daunting experience. You are engaging someone who will be part of your life, perhaps for months on end. They will be pulling your beloved home apart to make it bigger, better or more beautiful. If you make the right choice you may well be surprised at the lengths your builder goes to keep you a happy customer. Homeowners have written to me with many examples of builders going the extra mile. They have told me about simple services such as taking in the washing when it rains. Some clients have escaped the noise, dust and disruption, leaving their builder to look after the family pets. Including, in one case, their pot-bellied pig!

How can you make sure you get one of these builders from heaven? Well, you've already started. *Getting the Best from Your Builder* will help you with the essential steps of planning and preparation. It will guide you through managing the project and, if all doesn't go smoothly, it tells you how to deal with disputes and sort out problems. If you follow the advice in this book you won't go far wrong – and you'll be well on the way to finding a building angel.

Ian Davis MBA BEng. CEng. MICE
Director General
Federation of Master Builders

Introduction

Employing builders is generally regarded with trepidation by those who have never done it before, but also, more ominously, by many who have. Horror stories are common, from old ladies being conned out of their savings to unscrupulous roofers abandoning the job halfway through. But it doesn't have to be like that. With a bit of planning – and help from this book – employing builders can be like entering into any other professional relationship. Funds are exchanged for goods and services and there is a clear linear progression until the transaction is completed to the satisfaction of both parties.

For some building projects it may not be necessary to get the builders in at all. More than 60 per cent of households do some kind of DIY each year, according to a poll carried out for Black & Decker in 2002, so it may be feasible for you to tackle the job yourself. However, certain tasks will definitely require expert assistance from builders: an amorphous term that conjures up images of men in hard hats handling bricks and mortar, but in this book is taken to include decorators, plumbers, plasterers, carpenters, electricians, and affiliated trades that you might employ to perform work on your house.

Anything which involves getting planning permission, or interacting with other professions such as architects, structural engineers or district surveyors, is generally best left to experienced builders. Work on gas fittings or appliances carries a legal obligation to employ a registered CORGI (Council for Registered Gas Installers)* member. Water, electricity, bricks and mortar, major carpentry and plastering can become messy if not handled properly by experts. Unless you are a time-served DIYer, with a series of successfully completed projects behind you, it is best to leave jobs such as extensions, interfering with structural walls, putting in kitchens or bathrooms, loft and cellar conversions and conservatories to the professionals or a specialist firm.

Before the builder arrives: a seven-point survival plan

Whether you are a DIYer or one of the 40 per cent of people who at the end of the day would rather put their feet up than put up a shelf, this book is intended as a survival guide for the entire building process, from planning the job and finding a firm, to what to do if things go wrong (see Chapter 9). Building work is inherently unpredictable, and even if it goes well it will be stressful. There are usually too many variables for work to proceed exactly as planned, and so it rarely does. Stick to the seven-point plan below, and you can survive the whole experience.

1 Planning the job

Make a detailed plan of action in conjunction with the builder (see Chapter 4), breaking down the job into itemised phases with an agreed timescale and a total price, including materials, for each phase. Reputable contractors should produce a programme of events, and Quality Mark-registered builders (see page 157) are obliged to come up with an overall time or completion date. Depending on the nature of the job, you could ask when critical stages, such as breaking through into an existing house from an extension, will be carried out.

Living without essential facilities

If relevant, ask: 'How long, exactly, will I be without a bathroom or kitchen?' This is one of the most important things to ascertain at an early stage, because the inconvenience of being without these facilities is not to be taken lightly. Children might be better off staying with friends or relatives unless there is to be a guaranteed seamless transition from the old to the new facilities within a single day. In most cases this is definitely possible, though it is promised more often than it is achieved.

---

2 Ordering materials and appliances

Builders generally prefer to order their own materials, such as wood, sand and cement, and then charge the client at the end of the job. This can be beneficial, as they can usually buy materials at trade prices, though there is nothing to prevent them making a profit on the transaction. If you buy the materials yourself, make sure you have ordered everything on the builder's shopping list, or the job could be held up.

Appliances such as fridges, washing machines and cookers can have long delivery times; six to eight weeks is not uncommon, even from apparently well-stocked showrooms. The same applies to bathroom furniture, carpets and tiles, so make sure that absolutely everything you need for the job will be available when you need it, and not several weeks later. A finished bathroom just waiting for some taps to arrive from Italy is not a finished bathroom, but a major and costly inconvenience.

3 Have a very clear idea of what you want

These days there is so much choice in fixtures, fittings and finishes that almost any effect is achievable from a catalogue. It is a good idea to cut out pictures of what you want from magazines and brochures, so that you have tangible images of how the final result will look. Give your builder drawings and brief him with as much detail as possible about the effect you are after.

For any sizeable project, or for one that does not involve a designer and which you are unsure about, run through the options with your builder. It is important to do your homework properly. If you make any impractical or costly decisions, you may subsequently have to change some of your ideas to ones which are easier to implement. Even if compromise becomes inevitable, having a firm idea of the end point in your mind can stop the project from sliding into something unrecognisable from your original plan.

Avoid problems with custom-made fittings

If you are having things specially made or using non-standard fittings, extra care may be necessary. You should allow adequate time for the manufacture and arrival of specially crafted components, especially if they are being sent from overseas. It's also important to consider the whole picture. For example, non-standard kitchen units may not interact well with anything else in the kitchen, such as other units, worktops, dishwashers or cookers. Measure everything carefully and consider the appearance of new units to ensure that they will harmonise with other fittings.

---

4 Expect the unexpected

No building job ever goes entirely according to plan. Worst-case scenarios are discovering after work has started that the entire house needs underpinning, or has dry rot, or that the remains of a Roman Temple are lurking where you were going to put your patio.

The risk of mishaps is greatly reduced, however, if you have prepared adequately in advance and have a contingency plan for all eventualities. For example, do you need to obtain a parking permit for the builder's van? Will you need to hire a skip? (See Chapter 6, page 85.) Have you told the neighbours about the work? Have you agreed who will obtain Building Regulations approval?

Many difficulties can be foreseen. If you are doing work on a run-down old property, it is advisable to have damp, woodworm and rot surveys carried out to prevent unpleasant surprises later on. Perhaps you need to find out about soil conditions or where the drains run – in this case, your architect or surveyor (or the local Buildings Inspector) can help. In the case of a listed building, find out what developments the conservation officer will allow (see Chapter 2).

You could consider keeping a contingency sum of roughly 20 per cent of the value of the work aside to meet unexpected costs, though if you have done your homework you should find the job will be fairly straightforward and stay within expected parameters. It is a good idea to ask your builder for a fixed quote, rather than an estimate, to reduce uncertainty about the final cost of the work.

5 Keep it clean

A well-run site is as clean as possible at all times, and good builders tidy up as they go along, devoting at least half an hour at the end of each day to clearing up. Even so, many people are shocked at how much dirt can be generated, even by small jobs. Sanding, for instance, creates enormous amounts of dust, as does the removal of old plaster or the application of new. A simple task such as removing a fitted wardrobe may well involve all three of these processes.

By adopting the following tactics you can protect your home and surroundings from the worst of the mess.

- Buy plastic sheeting and tape to seal off unaffected areas, and treat the other side of it like a contaminated zone, vigilantly refusing to allow debris to pass through, or you will soon become enveloped by inexorably seeping dust. You can also put tape around doors, and block up the gap at the bottom with rolled-up newspaper or rags.
- Let your neighbours know about the work, because they will almost certainly be inconvenienced by noise or dirt. Check that piles of sand won't be trodden into anyone's lawn, for example.

6 Get everything out

Move out of the affected area anything that you don't want damaged, leaving only things which are destined for the skip, or are suitable for use in a war zone. If there is to be major work such as knocking down internal walls or stripping out a kitchen or bathroom, most people clear out everything down to the carpet or lino, but it can be worthwhile going further. Carpets may need to come up and go to the tip, and if there is floor sanding to be done, then the carpet grip around the edge of the room needs to be levered up with a crowbar. Doing the light stripping-out work yourself will save your builder charging half a day of his skilled time, and it will help you to adjust to the new conditions.

If you do decide to do any preliminary demolition yourself, make sure that you make a good job of it. Don't leave lots of mess lying around for the builders to clear up – no-one likes finishing someone else's job. And be sure to tell your contractor that you are going to do it yourself, or he'll build it into his costs anyway.

7 Prepare psychologically

Even the most carefully planned and executed building programme still has a slight feeling of the Wild West about it: the sense that almost anything can happen and that ultimately a measure of luck is required for it to go well. It is also noisy, dirty and costly, punctuated by enormous frustrations and disappointments – and it all takes place inside your house, which makes it very stressful. One of your main frames of reference, your home, will be torn apart and – you hope – reconfigured in front of you. There will be wheelbarrows in your living room and your hall will become a rat-run to the skip. But probably the worst aspect, psychologically, is the sense of an occupying force taking over for what can seem like an indefinite amount of time. Once the process is under way it is irreversible, so you feel totally dependent on the invaders to put it right again. It is generally safe to say that people who employ builders have a greater emotional attachment to the place where the work is to be carried out than do the builder and his employees, who look at a house in the same way that a pathologist looks at a body – able to envisage it reduced to its component pieces and laid out in front of them.

It is this difference in perspective which makes employing builders so potentially harrowing for the under-prepared; a mini life event, and not something to be undertaken lightly. If you are frantically busy at work, in poor health or otherwise vulnerable (for example, through bereavement, stress or pregnancy), think carefully about whether you need the rodeo bull of a building programme in your psychological china shop.

That frontier feeling can also be exhilarating at times, but even a decent builder will have a radically different take on the situation from you. 'Is the door wide enough to get the cement mixer in? Will I have to take the windows out? What's the wheelbarrow access like to the outside? Is there enough room to swing a shovel inside, or will we have to mix up cement and plaster outside? Where's the nearest café?' These are the questions the builder asks himself while he is sizing up the job. If you could fast-forward to a builder's-eye perspective of your living room, you would be enormously shocked. Builders are used to this maelstrom: you are probably not; so be warned, and prepare well using the tips in this guide.

Chapter 1

The planning stage

Most DIY and building work in the home is carried out to improve the living conditions in the house rather than increase its value, though if the work is properly planned and executed it should do both. Extra rooms, more space, an upgraded kitchen or bathroom, can all make your existing house seem a little bit more like your dream home to you, but also make it more appealing to future buyers.

This book covers projects which are too big or too complex to do yourself. It will help you plan what you need to do, establish whether you need permission and determine who you will need to help you to do it. If (as often happens with successful building work) you find yourself tempted to sell the house and move up a rung on the property ladder, it will also help you to do it all again.

Deciding what to do

Once you have identified which areas of your home you want to change or need to fix, the next step is to work out the best way to do it. The most common building projects can be divided into four main types, and this chapter gives a broad outline of what each involves, so that you can see whether it might be the solution to your problems. Any of them could fit your requirements individually but you may need to combine elements of several in order to get the result you want.

1 Changing the way you use existing rooms

Every room in your home currently has its own specific function. The house may have been built that way, or may have evolved its present layout as successive owners adapted it to suit their particular lifestyles. However, it need not stay as it is if it does not suit you. You can sometimes alter the function of individual rooms by simply moving the furniture around, although changes involving structural alterations will generally require getting the builders in. You could consider these options.

- Turn the main living room into a large kitchen-diner, leaving the existing dining room and kitchen to act as separate living rooms – one for home entertainment, perhaps, and one as a quiet room for reading or homework.
- Strip out the built-in kitchen units that you do not need so that you can create space in the room for a dining area, thus freeing the existing dining room to be used as an extra bedroom or living room.
- Fit out the boxroom as a second bathroom.

If a kitchen or bathroom is being created or relocated, the job may involve rerouting services, but this need not create any insurmountable problems. You may need Building Regulations approval for the work, however, and you should also check whether planning permission is required if you intend to work from home as this may constitute a change of use. (See Chapter 2 for more details on how the law affects building projects.)

2 Rearranging existing rooms

Changing the layout of your house is rather more radical than simply changing the use to which you put individual rooms. It may not significantly increase the floor area, but should help you to make better use of the existing space. Again, there are several options you could consider.

- Create fewer and larger rooms by knocking down internal walls. Making a through living-and-dining room is one popular alteration, but you could just as well combine the hall and living room (as long as you have a porch or lobby, so that the front door does not open directly into the converted room). The kitchen and dining room could be turned into a large kitchen-diner. Upstairs, two adjacent bedrooms could be converted into a large master bedroom, with spacious dressing and sitting areas.

- Change the size of adjacent rooms by removing the existing partition wall and then re-erecting it to provide one larger and one smaller room. This could allow you to convert, for example, two existing bedrooms into one large bedroom with an en suite bathroom.

- Create more smaller rooms by installing new partitions within large existing rooms, or by removing one partition between two rooms and erecting new partitions to divide up the resulting floor space into three separate areas instead of two. This latter option can also, of course, be used to create an extra bedroom or a second bathroom.

- Changing the position of door openings in internal walls may help create more useful space by altering traffic routes through the house, and allowing a more effective arrangement of the furniture against the walls. In through-rooms a second door could be blocked off. It may also be worth considering rehanging doors so that they open a different way, or using sliding doors instead of hinged ones in those situations in which the latter take up precious floor space.

- Changing the position of external doors may also be worth considering, especially those giving access to the side or rear of the house. An outside door in a kitchen may well provide a useful route to the garden, washing line or dustbin, but the traffic through the room seriously compromises the way in which the kitchen works. French or patio doors in a living or dining room will restrict the way in which the furniture can be arranged, whereas a window would give greater freedom.

- Moving the staircase may make better use of the space on the floor from which it rises, although this option may prove impossible in some house layouts. A spiral staircase may seem an obvious space-saver, but this rarely offers a significant gain in floor area, and can pose problems of safety and access for children, elderly people and furniture removers.

Rearranging existing space involves some structural work, especially if the walls you want to remove are load-bearing. You must always seek professional advice (see Chapter 3) if your plans affect a load-bearing wall. However, timber-framed partition walls can be removed and erected with relative ease.

3 Adapting existing unused space

Most houses have one major area of unused space within their existing outer shell: the loft. Others may have a basement or cellar, and some an integral or attached garage, which could all be converted into new living space without the need to build out the house itself.

Loft conversions

Converting the loft is one of the most popular large-scale home improvements, and, if it is well planned and executed, can be both a practical and an aesthetically pleasing addition to the house. Unfortunately, over the years, many houses and bungalows have been horribly disfigured by loft conversions that may well provide valuable extra living space on the inside but are eyesores when viewed from the outside.

The feasibility of a loft conversion depends on a number of factors. The first concerns the way in which the roof was constructed. If it was traditionally built with rafters, ridgepole, purlins and struts, the conversion will generally be fairly straightforward. However, professional advice is still always necessary to ensure that the roof structure will not be dangerously weakened by the conversion work.

If the roof was built using prefabricated trussed rafters, conversion will be more difficult, but not impossible.

The second factor concerns the potential room height. If your roof slope is particularly shallow, there may simply not be enough height in the existing roof space, and you would have to consider building above the roof ridge – something many local planning committees are most unlikely to allow.

The third factor concerns providing access to the conversion from the floor below. It may be possible to fit a new staircase above the existing stairwell, but the design of the roof may mean that there is not enough headroom unless a dormer is built over the stairwell. Siting the new staircase anywhere other than above the existing stairwell will take up valuable floor space, which is something to take into account when measuring the gain in net space that the conversion will provide.

Converting a loft is a potentially complex job, which most people prefer to leave to an architect and builder, or to a specialist firm.

You will need Building Regulations approval for a loft conversion, but planning permission is not generally required. (For more detailed information on loft conversions see page 113.)

Basement conversions

Nowadays houses are seldom built with basements, but they are a common feature in those (especially urban ones) built before World War I. Some basements were never intended to be more than small storage cellars, and were generally built beneath only part of the house. Others are more sizeable and can offer excellent potential for conversion.

As with loft conversions, three main factors will affect the feasibility of the conversion. The first is damp: however well the basement was built, it is below ground level and will therefore be at risk from water penetration from all sides, as well as from below, especially in areas where the water table has risen over the years. You may have to carry out extensive and potentially expensive damp-proofing treatment as the first stage of the conversion.

The second factor is ventilation, which must meet Building Regulations requirements if the basement is to be turned into habitable rooms: living rooms, dining rooms, bedrooms and kitchens you can eat in. You may be able to overcome the problem of lack of ventilation by creating an open well outside the basement and installing windows that open into it, but if this is not possible mechanical ventilation will have to be installed.

The third factor is lack of natural light. You may be able to provide this by installing openable windows for ventilation (see above), or by using paving-grade glass, or glass cobbles to make areas of the ceiling translucent. Otherwise, you will have to rely on artificial lighting. In this case, the uses to which you can put the basement rooms may be limited by the Building Regulations requirement for openable windows in habitable rooms.

Converting a basement may be relatively simple if the rooms are free from damp, but the job can be fairly complex and expensive if you intend to use them as habitable rooms. (For more detailed information on basement conversions see page 120).

Garage conversions

An integral or attached garage offers obvious potential for conversion into extra living space, especially if there is already an access door leading into it from the house. The amount of work involved in carrying out the conversion depends on the purpose to which you will put it.

If all you want is a workshop, a home for kitchen appliances such as the freezer, washing machine or tumble drier, or space to enable the children to play table tennis, then a coat of paint on the walls and an extension of your wiring and plumbing systems is all you need.

If it is to be a truly habitable room, however, the work involved will be much more extensive. The garage floor may not include a damp-proof membrane, and may be at a lower level than the house floor; it will also need insulating to bring it up to Building Regulations standards. Unless the garage is wholly within the house, the external walls will be of single-thickness brickwork, so they will have to be both insulated and dry-lined. In an attached garage, you will also have to put in a ceiling with insulation above it; the ceiling of an integral garage should already be well insulated. Most garage conversions turn the garage-door opening into a large front window.

You may also want to add other windows to the side or back walls, especially if you intend to partition the space within the conversion. If there is no access door, you will have to create a new opening at a convenient point in the house wall, which may take up space within the house itself.

Servicing the new rooms

Having successfully converted unused space, you will have to extend the house's wiring to provide better lighting and some power points, and will have to consider how to heat the new rooms. If plumbing facilities are required, you will have to extend supply pipes and make arrangements for getting rid of waste water.

---

4 Adding new living space

If you need more living space than is actually available within your home, and none of the previous options solves your problem, you have little choice but to build on. A full-blown extension of one or two storeys is the obvious choice, although adding a conservatory at the back or side of the house is also a popular way of gaining an additional living room or recreational area.

Home extensions

How you extend your home will depend on several factors. The most critical is the availability of space on the site for the projected extension, and it is generally obvious what the options are. The most likely is an extension at the back of the house, but it can be very difficult to make the new work look like part of the original building – the ideal of any home extension. If there is space at the side of the house, an extension here can be blended with the existing structure much more easily, especially if it is given a pitched, rather than a flat, roof. Front extensions are generally not allowed by the planning authorities, unless the house is set well back from the road or is behind the building line with which the fronts of the neighbouring properties are aligned.

Assuming that you have room on site to extend your home, you must next decide what sort of extra space you need, since this will dictate the type of extension that you build. A single-storey rear extension is ideal for extending a kitchen or living room, but if you need more bedrooms or an extra bathroom, a two-storey extension is a must (unless, of course, you live in a bungalow). This will generally be a brand-new structure, also providing extra ground-floor living space or an integral garage, although in some cases you may be able to add a storey to an existing side garage or single-storey extension if the foundations and structure are strong enough. When planning a two-storey extension, you will have to pay particular attention to organising the access arrangements in order to minimise any undue loss of space in the existing house.

Once you have decided what to build and where to build it, you can start to plan the project in detail. The size of the job means that you will almost certainly need professional assistance from a designer, such as an architect, building surveyor or architectural consultant (see Chapter 3). Unless the work counts as permitted development, you will also need to apply for planning permission, and you will in any case need Building Regulations approval. (For more detailed information on home extensions see page 125.)

Conservatories

Conservatories have become one of the most popular types of major domestic building projects in recent years, reviving a construction that first became fashionable in Victorian times. In their current reincarnation they have evolved from the humble sunroom – essentially a lean-to greenhouse – into a variety of highly elaborate styles and shapes that can blend in with any type of house design.

The modern conservatory is basically a modular building, consisting of a series of prefabricated glazed units which are assembled to form a perimeter wall that may be square, rectangular, or with angled corners in hexagonal or octagonal shapes. Double glazing is essential if you expect to be able to use the room all year round, as is good insulation in any solid-wall areas.

The roof is no longer the heavy structure of the traditional conservatories, with their panels of wired glass. Modern plastics technology has produced the perfect roofing material, called polycarbonate: a light, rigid sheet, with a box-section structure, which is available in twin- and triple-wall versions. The air trapped within the box sections acts as an excellent insulator, and the lightness of the material, coupled with its strength, means that the roof structure can also be comparatively light in weight and unobtrusive in appearance.

A conservatory is usually sited at the back of the house, for obvious reasons: it will act as an extension to the main living areas, and the back is where space is most likely to be available. However, if there is room, it could also be sited at the side of the house, and such a position will maximise the effects of the available sunlight.

Adding a conservatory is generally one of the least disruptive types of building project to carry out, since all the construction work takes place outside the house. Most conservatories are built against walls which already have either an existing door opening, or a window that can be easily enlarged to form one. Once the base for the structure is in place, the building can be erected and weatherproofed in a day or so, and is then ready for immediate use.

Most people buy a conservatory from a specialist supplier who also carries out all the installation work, but an alternative is to order the components and assemble the building yourself.

Conservatories count as home extensions for planning purposes and so permission must be sought if you exceed the permitted development allowance (see page 32). In England, Wales and Northern Ireland conservatories are exempt from Building Regulations control provided they do not exceed 30sq m (about 325sq ft) in area. (For more detailed information on conservatories see page 120.)

Improving service amenities and energy efficiency

Reorganising the existing plumbing arrangements may require Building Regulations approval if this involves relocating waste water disposal, while changes affecting water supply must comply with water by-laws.

Improving your home's wiring and lighting may involve the extension of existing circuits, the provision of new ones, and even complete rewiring if the system is old and cannot stand the extra load. The work needs no official permission (except in Scotland), but should be carried out to Wiring Regulations standards – see page 34. Bear in mind that the installation of new heating appliances needs Building Regulations approval.

Energy-efficient measures such as incorporating improved thermal insulation, improving draught-proofing and providing controlled ventilation should be part and parcel of many of your projects, whether you are converting the loft, fitting double glazing or replacing doors and windows. These features will all have long-term, cost-saving or comfort-improving benefits. New building work will have to meet the thermal insulation requirements of the Building Regulations. *The Which? Guide to the Energy-Saving Home* explains what you need to consider.

Weighing up the pros and cons

With all potential home improvement projects it is worth asking at the outset: is the work really a good idea? Will it increase the value of the property by more than the cost of the work? Or might it actually reduce the appeal of the property? You may want a Californian-style underlit jacuzzi sunk into your patio, but other potential buyers of similar properties might regard it as a ludicrous eyesore which will need to be taken out – so in fact it may simultaneously narrow the band of appeal and reduce the value of the house. A survey conducted by the Woolwich Building Society in 2001 concluded that while installing central heating and refurbishing the kitchen and bathroom would add value to your property, other projects, such as adding a conservatory or converting the loft, were less likely to recoup their considerable cost.

You should also consider the knock-on effects of the work once it is completed. Will it affect the amount of light available, or create extra traffic in certain areas of the house? Will it cover a manhole? (For more on building laws see Chapter 2.)

Think about practicalities too. Will your existing fuse box be able to cope with the demand from extra sockets, or will your wiring need to be upgraded?

Soil stacks – the large-diameter waste pipes from a toilet – are difficult to relocate, and generally run down one side of a house. If you are proposing to add a toilet on the other side, having a stack running through the house may not be practical.

Many schemes are possible, but not all are necessarily advisable. With the help of this book, you should be able to assess the pros and cons of major projects, such as kitchen refurbishment, loft conversion, conservatory installation or a two-storey extension. If you decide to go ahead it will help you ensure that they are completed smoothly, economically and with the minimum of disruption.

Chapter 2

Builders and the law

When undergoing building work, it is best to understand the legal basics. As well as protecting you from the worst excesses of bad builders, the law also imposes certain responsibilities on the homeowner, including following the Building Regulations, applying for planning consent for projects where necessary and keeping obligations towards builders. This chapter discusses the building laws that can apply and considerations that can protect you when drawing up a contract.

Sometimes frustratingly, but probably fortunately, we do not have free rein on what we can do to our homes. The Town and Country Planning Acts and the Building Act have much to say about what is permissible, and although there is sometimes scope for negotiation, navigation of this particular labyrinth might best be achieved by your project manager, if you have one (see Chapter 5), who should be well-versed in building laws and procedures. He may deem it necessary to employ a specialist planning consultant, though these are usually necessary only on more complicated commercial jobs.

If your project looks as though it might require planning permission and/or Building Regulations approval, contact your local authority's Planning and/or Building Control departments, which are separate but often good at working together. They are often combined in one department called Development Control.

Some properties are further restricted as far as development or use is concerned by covenants in the title deeds. A covenant may, for instance, stipulate that certain alterations or additions shall not be made or only with the consent of the person who sold the land on which the property was built. (Some covenants cannot be enforced but, if in doubt, consult a solicitor.) Also, mortgage deeds normally have a clause stipulating that the building society's (or other lender's) approval must be obtained for any proposed alterations to the house. If a property is leasehold, the landlord's consent will probably be required.

Planning permission

Planning permission is about *what* you can do with your home – whether it is building an extension or converting part of your home for business use. Some amount of home extension is allowed under the Town and Country Planning Acts (see box), but you are likely to need planning permission if you want to:

- extend your home forwards or upwards
- build extensions of more than a certain size
- change the use of your home in any way, including converting it into flats.

If you are in any doubt about whether you need to apply for permission, then you should ask. If the authorities discover that you have done something without the prior necessary approval, they have it in their power to make you apply for permission retrospectively. They can also issue an enforcement notice, requiring you to restore a building to its former condition or its former use (a notice has to be issued within four years of the work being completed, or it cannot be legally enforced, unless the building is listed).

Generally the authorities prefer the latter option, because they don't want to set a precedent of allowing people to disregard the procedures. You may also be prosecuted and fined and, if you fight the judgement all the way and lose, you may ultimately have to witness the extension you put up at your own expense being demolished by bulldozers paid for with your own tax. You can get a leaflet *Planning: A Guide for Householders* from your local council which explains the basic rules. It is also downloadable from the website of the Office of the Deputy Prime Minister (ODPM)★ at *www.odpm.gov.uk*.

Exemptions from planning permission

It is always best to check with your local authority before embarking on any kind of building project. However, certain additions or alterations to your property can be carried out without planning permission as long as your home is not listed, in a Conservation Area, an Area of Outstanding Natural Beauty, a National Park, or the Norfolk or Suffolk Broads.

In England and Wales, things that may be exempt include:

- **a conservatory**, provided it is under 30 sq m (except for regulations regarding glazing)
- **domestic TV and radio aerials** – though you may need permission for some satellite dishes (ask your council for the leaflet on these)
- **extensions** (including conservatories and garages closer than 5 m to the house) are allowed as long as they don't increase the volume of the house by more than your 'permitted development rights' (see box below). Also, watch out for the boundary with your neighbours; if an extension (or conservatory or large garage) is closer to the boundary than 2 m, there will be height restrictions to prevent it blocking out their sun
- **a fuel oil storage tank**, provided it is less than 3,500 litres in capacity, no more than 3 m high and no closer to any highway than the house (unless it is at least 20 m away). Note that you always need permission for an LPG (Liquefied Petroleum Gas) tank
- **a garden wall or fence**, provided it is not more than 1 metre high along the boundary with a road, or 2 m high in other places. Hedges, however, are almost always exempt, unless there is a condition attached to the original planning permission for your property which restricts the planting of hedges or trees
- **hard-standing areas** – which means driveways, patios or just areas of your garden which you would like to give over to concrete or stone – are generally allowed, but you will need permission if you want to make new or wider access for your driveway on to a trunk or other classified road. You need the separate approval of the Highways Department of your council if a new driveway would cross a pavement or a verge

- **internal alterations** or work not affecting the external appearance of the house
- **a porch,** as long as it is more than 2 m from the road or footpath, is less than 3 m high and does not occupy more than 3 sq m of floor space.
- **roof extensions and loft conversions** These are allowed if they don't increase the volume of the house by more than 50 cu m (40 cu m for a terraced house).
- **roof windows** – i.e. those lying flat with the roof surface (often colloquially known as 'Velux' windows, after the main make). Note, however, that dormer windows (which project vertically from a sloping roof) are not generally permitted if they are facing a road.
- **a shed,** as long as it is not put up in front of the building line (the wall of the house facing the highway) and the height does not exceed 4m if it has a ridged roof, or 3m if the roof is flat.
- **a swimming pool** As long as it doesn't take up more than half of your garden you can generally have a swimming pool, if you have obtained your water company's consent and you can afford it – be prepared for a huge increase in your water rates. A little pool, perhaps solar-heated to reduce the long-term costs, and maybe even with a water-jet to swim against, could dramatically improve the value of your house, your standard of living, your cardiovascular fitness and your morale all at the same time.

Applying for planning permission

If you think you might need planning permission, contact the planning department of your local authority – and ask for an application form, if necessary. They will tell you what the fee is and how many copies of the form you need to send back. Prior to applying, you could seek advice from a planning consultant or a building surveyor who may assist you with the application and plans. Sometimes, builders may be able to provide this service, but usually they will tell you to consult a surveyor. One of the advantages in employing local surveyors is that they will be familiar with the criteria adopted by the local planning authority. This may well save you the disappointment of a refusal or possible changes.

Normally, you will make a full application, but sometimes you might want to make an outline application – to find out what the authority thinks of your ideas before making detailed plans (you will still need to make a full application later).

After acknowledging your application, the council places your application on the Planning Register, where it can be inspected by any interested parties. It may also notify your neighbours or put up a notice on or near your house.

The application should be decided within eight weeks unless you give written consent to extend this period. The council must decide whether or not there are any good planning reasons for refusing consent – it will not reject a proposal simply because many people oppose it. They may approve it in full, reject it or grant permission with certain conditions.

If permission is granted (with or without conditions), you must start work within the specified time limit; if it is rejected (or not decided within eight weeks) you have the right of appeal to the Secretary of State or you can resubmit a modified application free of charge within 12 months.

Building Control will issue a final certificate (as well as a Building Control approval certificate – known as a Notice of Passing of Plans). If the construction does not comply with the Regulations, the owner will be prosecuted.

Building Regulations

The Building Regulations – created under The Building Act – are about *how* you carry out building work to your home, whether or not planning permission is required. With a few exemptions – most conservatories and porches, for example – everything that affects the health and safety of the people living inside the house needs to meet the requirements of the Building Regulations. The Regulations are also concerned with energy conservation and with means of escape in the event of fire, and cover access for the disabled.

Since 1985, the Regulations have given only general require-ments. All they have to say on ventilation, for example, is that 'there shall be adequate means of ventilation provided for people in the building'. How this is interpreted in practice is up to the Building Control Officer concerned. You can choose any method you like for meeting the general requirement, but he is much more likely to be convinced that it meets the Building Regulations if you follow the specific advice contained in the Approved Documents (one for each part of the Regulations) – see below. These give examples of how you prove that the building will comply with the Regulations.

The Regulations may seem restrictive at times, but because the UK has some of the highest standards of controls on building development in the world, you are unlikely to buy a house which is fundamentally dangerous to live in, unless it has been illegally developed or neglected for a significant length of time. In the latter case the symptoms should be obvious – look for faded paint, worn gutter boards, large damp patches on walls or floors, missing tiles and perhaps a scary-looking fuse box from the middle of the last century. In the case of illegal developments, the problems are not always so easy to detect. It could be that you first find out about one when a floor caves in, or you are stuck in a fire in the loft with no way out.

Note that the majority of Building Regulations are not retrospective, so you can generally replace like with like. This does not apply to things which affect energy use – so replacement windows, for example, have to meet the requirements of the latest Regulations, not the ones that were in force when the windows were first put in. You can get *Building Regulations: An Explanatory Booklet* from your local council (or it is downloadable from the ODPM★ website – see above).

The 13 'Approved Documents' for the Building Regulations in England and Wales (17 in Scotland) are published by the government, although some have been produced by private organisations. The Documents are issued by the Office of the Deputy Prime Minister★, and copies are available from The Stationery Office★ (or downloadable from the ODPM website).

At the time of writing the Scottish Executive is consulting on major changes to the Scottish Building Regulations, and the government is keeping a watching brief with a view to seeing which aspects of the Scottish Regulations could influence policy in England and Wales.

Your builder must comply with the Building Regulations, and if he does not, this may be taken as evidence that he has not built in a workmanlike manner. Additionally, he may be in breach of an implied legal obligation to use reasonable care and skill or to undertake the work in a workmanlike manner, depending on whether it is a complete new build/conversion or a home improvement. The builder is under an implied duty in law not to complete the work in a way which contravenes the Building Regulations.

Building Control

Building Regulations are enforced by your local authority's Building Regulations Department, sometimes called the Building Control Department, and generally known in the trade as Building Control. Building Control sounds more Orwellian, which is appropriate because as well as calling in at critical stages such as foundation laying, steel supports being concealed and, always, the drains going in, Building Control may also visit the site unannounced to inspect safety standards. In some areas, Building Control Officers are known as Building Inspectors, but they do the same job.

The Building Act allows for building control to be exercised by an independent Approved Inspector, but the vast majority of work is still handled by local authority Building Control Officers.

Applying for Building Regulations approval

In England and Wales there are two ways to apply for the approval of Building Control:

- you give the council a Building Notice with a relatively rudimentary drawing and outline of the works. No formal approval is given, though more information may later be requested
- you submit your full plans for inspection and receive written confirmation of the council's decision.

Although the full plans route takes longer, this method is preferable, because any requested alterations are definitely best dealt with at this stage. The full plans method also has the advantage of ensuring that Building Control feel fully informed, and so might be inclined to make fewer site visits. You also have the reassurance of approval in writing – always useful when you come to sell the house.

Whichever route you follow – Building Notice or full plans – you can start work two clear days after depositing your application and giving a 'commencement notice'. You will need to notify the council as you reach certain stages in the work. The two methods are explained in detail in the *Manual to the Building Regulations,* also available from The Stationery Office* or downloadable from the ODPM* website. The two methods generally involve the same fee.

How far you can develop your house

Your permitted development rights are:

- *for most houses* 15 per cent of the volume (up to a maximum of 115 cu m) or 70 cu m (whichever is greater)
- *for terraced houses and those in Conservation Areas or areas of Outstanding Natural Beauty, National Parks, the Norfolk or Suffolk Broads a lower limit applies* – 10 per cent of the volume (up to a maximum of 115 cu m) or 50 cu m (whichever is greater).

Volume is measured externally and calculated against the size of the house when it was first built, or as it stood on 1 July 1948, if it was built before then. These are 'once-and-for-all' allowances, so it could easily be that your house's allowance has already been used up. Your local authority should have details of the original size of the building.

In Scotland, a building warrant from Building Control is required. This is similar to the 'full plans' route in England and Wales.

Listed buildings

Listed buildings are divided into three grades: Grade I, Grade II* and Grade II. English Heritage* is the body that advises the government on listing, but the Department of Media, Culture and Sport makes the final decision. Once a building is listed, its owners will deal with English Heritage.

Grade I

A Grade I-listed building is considered to be of 'exceptional' architectural or historical interest. This may include examples of craftsmanship or other decorative techniques, or 'group value' where it is part of a series of buildings designed to sit together, as in a close, or even a whole village.

Although a Grade I-listed building can be a status symbol for the owner, it can also be extremely costly to maintain, as English Heritage★ has the right to insist that certain works are carried out at your expense in order to maintain the condition and character of the building. It is not unheard of for orders to be made to demolish some offending add-ons which have been detected and diagnosed as inappropriate; restoring the building to its original use is likely to be a condition when you purchase a Grade I-listed house. All works subject to Listed Building Consent are VAT exempt. Contact English Heritage for more details.

Grade II*
Buildings in this category have the same features as a Grade I building, but are considered 'particularly' rather than 'exceptionally' important.

Grade II
Grade II status is awarded to buildings which are of 'special interest' and which warrant 'every effort to preserve them'. In practice this can mean that they have a rarity value, great age, an unusual location, or are classic examples of a type.

Grade II-listed buildings are reasonably common in the residential sector (this may include structures such as walls and outbuildings within the boundaries of the property that is listed). Although the rules governing alterations are lighter than for Grade I, all internal and external alterations still require the approval of English Heritage, or possibly your local authority if it has acquired this overseeing role. Increasingly, English Heritage★ and other planning authorities are taking a strict conservationist stance with regard to the nation's architectural heritage, which is, after all, a finite resource. You may find that you encounter serious opposition even to changing the use of a room, or moving an internal non-structural partition wall. However, some people find that on the ground their local Conservation Officer is flexible and open-minded about internal alterations and may allow you to, say, remove internal walls, change the position of doorways or move a bathroom to another room.

Applying for listed building consent

If you are planning alterations you should approach English Heritage* or your local authority. Obtaining listed building consent (LBC) is generally considered to be more problematic than getting planning permission. The process is supposed to take roughly eight weeks, but it can take longer. This may be something to farm out to a specialist, such as a local planning consultant who has specific experience in negotiating for local listed building consent

---

Conservation Areas

The Office of the Deputy Prime Minister's planning department has responsibility for Conservation Areas, defined as 'areas of special architectural or historical interest, the character or appearance of which it is desirable to preserve or enhance'. Such areas are designated by local planning authorities and are often, though not always, centred around listed buildings. This means that even if your house is not listed, if it is in a Conservation Area then planners are likely to want to keep things exactly the way they are. Dormer windows may be forbidden unless a very good case can be made – for example, most of your neighbours already have them – and even features such as hedges and trees are covered, which can affect your planning (although a tree can be cut down if it is in a dangerous state or causes a hazard).

Sometimes, a local authority may issue an 'Article 4 Direction' in a Conservation Area which, in effect, removes some or all of your permitted development rights (see box on page 32), meaning you will need planning permission for a wider range of improvements.

Services and utilities

Wiring regulations

In the UK, domestic wiring is covered by the Wiring Regulations, but these currently do not have the force of law, except in Scotland where they form part of the Scottish Building Regulations. This means that in England and Wales anyone who thinks they can install or fix wiring can have a go. Fortunately most people realise that major jobs are best left to a qualified electrician who is required to follow the regulations. Wiring must comply with the British Standard, and is likely to be included in the Building Regulations at some future date.

Electricity supply companies can refuse to supply what they consider to be an unsafe installation, and they also have the right to inspect any installation which they suspect may be unsafe.

The *Which? Book of Wiring and Lighting*, from Which? Books*, explains how to carry out a variety of jobs in accordance with professional standards.

Water

Whilst drainage from properties is covered by the Building Regulations, anything to do with the supply of water is covered by The Water Supply (Water Fittings) Regulations – in Scotland the Regulations are virtually identical, though they are called bylaws there. The Regulations are enforced by your local water company. They have the force of law and you can be fined if you contravene them.

You must give your water company notice (and receive its consent) before building a swimming pool or making certain alterations or additions to your plumbing installation, especially those with the potential to contaminate the water supply through back-siphonage. This can happen if there is a sudden demand for water on a large scale elsewhere – nearby factory use, for example, or fire engines taking water to fight a local fire – which creates suction in taps and outlets in a wide area. So if, for example, you have the shower head on your mixer tap sitting in a full bath, some of that dirty bath water could be sucked through the shower head and back into the clean supply. This is why your water company must be informed before you install any appliance that has the potential for creating back-siphonage, such as a bidet with an ascending spray or flexible hose – unless the work is carried out by an 'approved contractor'. Normally, a Water Inspector will visit your home, but if you do not hear within ten days of the correct documentation having been received, permission to do the work is deemed to have been given and work may proceed. The Water Regulations are not easy to read, although a guide is published by the Water Regulations Advisory Scheme (WRAS)*.

Gas

The Gas Safety (Installation and Use) Regulations insist that all work on gas pipes, fittings and appliances including boilers, gas fires and gas cookers must be carried out by a registered, qualified installer. Contact CORGI (the Council for Registered Gas Installers)* to find a CORGI-registered installer in your area. Operatives carry identification cards that list the areas of gas work the holder is certified to carry out. If in doubt, you can check an installer's credentials directly with CORGI.

Where the works are to be supervised by a building inspector, then it is the builder's or building owner's responsibility to ensure compliance. A notice must be given to Building Control so that the inspector can inspect the works. Such notice has to be given by a person carrying out building work, which includes the builder as well as the building owner.

If you become a landlord, it is your responsibility to ensure that all gas fittings are certified safe by CORGI, which requires annual checks.

Any person who contravenes the Building Regulations is liable upon summary conviction to a fine of up to £5,000 and to further fines of £50 per day for every day of default.

A local authority has statutory power to order the removal or alteration of any work contravening the Regulations. Others have the right to apply for an injunction to secure compliance.

Contracts

Letters of Agreement

For small-scale improvements you may need only a simple letter of agreement, signed by both parties. This should cover the following points:

- a brief description of the job to be done
- the agreed price for the work (with a copy of the contractor's original quotation attached to the back of the letter)
- the person responsible for obtaining any necessary official approval for the work

- the agreed starting and finishing dates; the phrase 'time is of the essence' should be included if meeting the latter is important
- how you will pay for the work, and, if you have agreed to make staged payments, when they will fall due
- whether any part of the payment can be withheld in the event of a dispute arising between the parties, or on completion of the job, as a retainer against the cost of rectifying any defects found in the work.

Quotations as Contracts

Some contractors will supply quotations that are detailed enough to act as contracts, and may have the contractor's standard terms and conditions printed on the back of the quotation. These are especially common among firms offering package deals on home improvements such as conservatories, kitchen refits and replacement windows. Always read the terms carefully before you sign: they are often more for the supplier's benefit than yours, and once you have signed the document you are bound by them.

An exception to this involves contracts for products such as replacement windows and new kitchens that are ordered in very specific circumstances. If the seller calls at your home without invitation, or visits you by appointment after making an unsolicited telephone call, and you then place an order for goods during that visit, you have some rights of cancellation, even if you have signed a contract. These are as follows:

- written notice of these rights must be given to you when you sign the order; if it is not, the seller cannot enforce the contract
- you then have a 'cooling-off' period of seven days, within which you can cancel the order by writing to the seller. Any deposit that you paid when you signed the order must be returned to you in full.

According to the provisions of the Consumer Credit Act 1974, you may also be able to cancel a signed contract if you agreed to take credit to pay for the work. If the seller offers you credit directly, or acts as a broker by arranging credit for you with a professional lender, you can generally cancel the contract if all the following points apply:

- the goods/services cost between £100 and £30,000 and the amount of credit is less than £25,000.
- your house is not used as security for the loan
- you signed the credit agreement after discussing it face to face with the seller
- you signed it somewhere other (usually in your own home) than at the seller's or lender's premises.

You will be given a copy of the credit agreement when you sign it, and you must receive a second copy by post a few days later. These must both set out your rights of cancellation. You then have five days in which to decide whether you want to cancel the contract, starting from the date on which you received the second copy. Cancel the contract in writing, sending your letter to the seller by recorded delivery so that you have proof that it has been sent and received. A certificate of posting is important as the cancellation takes place as soon as you post the letter.

Making a contract

A contract is basically an agreement which is recognised by law. A contract may be made by word of mouth or in writing. A written contract is preferable as it provides clear evidence of what the parties intended at the time. The terms of verbal contracts can be difficult to prove. Written evidence is easier to prove than 'his word against mine' in the event of a dispute.

Building contracts are often complex documents. They should provide a contract for the builder's services entailing payment related to progress, a start and end date, arrangements for possession of the site, insurance, and variations or changes to the works. They may involve not just the employment of a builder but also a contract administrator – whether an architect or a quantity surveyor. They also involve the procurement of materials and supply of goods which may be converted to become part of the property in the building. All these matters, as well as facilities to extend the time required for the builder to complete and damages to compensate the building owner if the work is delayed, should ideally be included in the drafting of the contract.

Formal contracts

A formal written contract must be the preferred course for the homeowner because it provides clarity and certainty compared to recollections of various conversations at different times. A building project is too costly an expenditure to leave to recollection and impressions of who said what to whom. It is unwise to risk undertaking a building project on a mere oral contract. At the very least, you should get the basics committed to writing, i.e. what is to be done and how much it will cost. The project is far too important to be left to doubt, and to be left to pure reliance on the builder to perform (unless you are qualified in building surveying or architecture and engineering or law). Seek professional advice if in any doubt, otherwise you could find yourself spending exorbitant amounts of money and ending up in a dispute about unfilled expectations. What you want and what the builder can do may be completely different perceptions. What you want to aim at is narrowing perception to the realistic.

You should take advice about the precise form and wording of the contract. You may wish to insert particular clauses to deal with certain matters such as disputes. See page 42.

Offer and acceptance

A contract consists of these essential elements:

- **offer and acceptance** The agreement to do a certain amount of work, within a specified timescale
- **consideration** The money you agree to pay the builder
- **intention to create legal relations** A demonstration that the parties intend a binding legal relationship
- **capacity** Parties must be over the age of 18 and of sound mind
- **lawful objects** The objects (purposes) of the contract must be lawful otherwise the contract will not be enforceable.

There must be a clear offer and an unconditional acceptance of the offer. When you want to create a contract, seek tenders from various builders so that you can compare rates and prices for the work. Otherwise you will have no idea whether the price is reasonable or not. You should also seek advice about where to find reputable builders in your area and ideally find a good local one who has been in business for a reasonable time and is not likely to go out of business. You should invite tenders from at least three or four builders and compare. If in any doubt seek professional advice.

You can elect to have plans drawn up by a surveyor or architect and then submit them to a builder to price the work or ask the builder to prepare them. He will usually use his own surveyor and charge you for that. Your surveyor can prepare a Schedule of Works (see box on page 43) or specification which the builder will price. The specification is simply a list of building items – for example foundations, walls or windows – which are identified as part of the building and separately priced for materials and labour.

The tender you send out is what is termed an invitation to negotiate – it is not an offer. It does, however, become an offer in law when you accept the builder's price for the work. It may then be said there is a binding agreement on the terms agreed, subject to a formal contract being drawn up.

Appointing an administrator

It is advisable in some projects to employ a project manager, who may be an architect or surveyor (see Chapter 5). This person effectively stands between yourself and the builder so that as your agent he can ensure the builder maintains progress, that the work is in accordance with the contract, that payments are properly certified and works valued, that you do not overpay, and that the works are completed in a reasonable time. This saves you having any confrontations with the builder, which can be harmful. It should also save you time and money in certain types of project.

Contract suppliers

'There was this instant mutual trust', 'I liked his face,' and 'He seemed honest' are all reasons people have given for employing a builder, and all are harmless enough criteria in their own right – as long as they are backed up with a good, sound, watertight contract. These days, drawing up a contract need not involve a notary or solicitor; you can go and buy one from a contract supplier.

The most commonly used supplier of contracts to the building trade and its customers is the Joint Contracts Tribunal (JCT)*, which was formed by a reputable group of interested parties including the Royal Institute of British Architects (RIBA)*, the Royal Institution of Chartered Surveyors (RICS)*, the British Property Federation* and the Association of Consulting Engineers★ – among others – in order to introduce recognisable and reliable standard contracts for the industry. And with the advent of the JCT, they have largely succeeded.

The JCT Minor Works Agreement (MW98) is suitable for most relatively straightforward domestic jobs up to a value of around £150,000. One of the criteria for using the MW98 is that 'the work involved is simple in character', so for a larger and more complicated job you may require the Intermediate Form of Building Contract (IFC98), which provides 'more detailed provisions and more extensive control procedures' than the MW98.

For very simple jobs, the JCT★ also offers the HO/RM Contract for Home Repairs and Maintenance (not for use in Scotland). This includes provision for the price being either a lump sum or based on an hourly rate, but provides for payment only on completion of the work. For this reason it is not suitable for jobs which are expected to last longer than four weeks, and is generally used for much shorter works.

Other contract suppliers include the Federation of Master Builders (FMB)★. Its contract for domestic work has won an award from the Plain English Campaign. There are now four FMB minor works contracts to choose from, including one for Scotland. The Quality Mark★ scheme has simple forms of contract for minor home repair and improvement work.

There are certain advantages in using one of the Standard Form Contracts. For example, you get:

- an industry-wide accepted form with a fixed lump sum price
- a procedural recognised framework for the builder, contract administrator and building owner
- certainty as to start and completion dates
- a certain balance of risk allocation between the parties.

Disadvantages of the Standard Form Contracts are as follows:

- the forms are a compromise of rights between the various institutional organisations, which publish the forms primarily for the benefit of their members in the industry not the consumer
- some procedures provide a mechanism for unreasonable money claims or extension of time claims by builders

- in practice the fixed lump sum invariably becomes a varied sum, seldom lowered but often increased.

For these reasons, homeowners may require independent professional advice about the type of contract required and any special terms.

What to include in a contract

In general your contract should establish the following points :

- the name of the contractor who will carry out the work
- the sum total of the fee, plus the frequency and conditions of interim payments (such as the amount of work that must be completed before payment is due), and the amount of retention (usually 5 per cent) – a sum of money which is not paid until all defective work has been put right
- the start and completion dates, with provisions outlined for damages payable in the event of 'unreasonable' delays (not all builders will agree to this, however, particularly on smaller contracts.)
- that any variations to the work, including to costings and any projected alteration to the completion date, should be authorised in writing before being carried out
- that the contractor carries appropriate public liability, employer's and bankruptcy insurance (see page 44)
- limitation (The law allows you up to six years to sue for breach of contract, and six years to sue for negligence. If the contract is by way of deed (under seal) then the time in which to sue is 12 years from the date of breach or the effective date the damage was suffered. This can be extended to up to 15 years under the Latent Damage Act, depending on the circumstances.)
- arrangements for the resolution of disputes.

The contract should include certain express terms to the effect that the contractor will:

- execute the work with reasonable care and skill, in a workman-like and competent manner in accordance with the schedule of works, drawings and other contract documents including the conditions of contract
- use materials which are of satisfactory quality and fit for their purpose

- regularly attend the site and diligently carry out the work
- keep the site tidy and dispose of rubbish
- comply with applicable health and safety and statutory obligations
- confirm he has appropriate 'all risks' and public liability insurance to cover the foreseeable value of claims in the future
- provide guarantees for certain manufactured items.

Sometimes builders try to cap the time you have to raise any defects with them. They shouldn't do this as you cannot exclude someone's statutory rights. You should, however, bring to the builder's attention the defects as soon as possible. If, for example, your delays result in the deterioration of your property then the contractor may not be liable for your additional losses that result.

In addition to the terms you expressly agree, the Supply of Goods and Services Act 1982 and the Defective Premises Act 1972 also imply specific terms into your contract. (See Chapter 9, page 141 for more details.)

The contract documents for major works will include the contract itself, as well as the tender drawings, the specification (a written brief from the architect or engineer outlining the precise nature of the work to be carried out and the materials to be used),

---

The Schedule of Works

This is a document which provides an overview of the entire job, broken into simple stages detailing payment and completion schedules for each phase. It is essentially a précis of the specification with some additional information, ideally contained on a single sheet of A4 to make it more user-friendly for the non-expert (i.e. you). An example might be:

Weeks 1–2 (August 7–21) Site preparation, plumbing installation.
Week 3 (August 21–28) Bathroom completed; first payment due.
Week 4 (August 28–September 4) Preliminary work on kitchen begins.

This way, if you get to September and the bathroom is not finished but the builder is still asking for payment, you have an at-a-glance guide with which to make a judgement.

---

and the priced Schedule of Works describing the work to be carried out and the price for each item of work. Copies of the contract are signed and exchanged with the builder, and you are then both bound to abide by it. You can make clear any detailed requirements you have in this documentation, even if they are in the form of a handwritten plan.

Insurance Backed Guarantees (IBGs)

Even the best builders can occasionally 'go bust' through no fault of their own, or be unable to complete the job owing to ill health or accidents. This can be difficult for everyone involved, particularly when you have laid out large sums of money and there is rain coming in through a hole where your roof used to be. The only way to be absolutely sure that this doesn't happen to you is to go for an Insurance Backed Guarantee scheme, or IBG. It is important to distinguish between these schemes and builders who simply advertise 'all work guaranteed'. This affords no protection if the builder goes bankrupt. There are a number of building industry guarantee schemes which may be worth joining if you are planning a long and involved project, or one in which a delay would constitute a serious problem. You may find that you are covered for the completion of unfinished work if the contractor concerned is a member of a trade association, but you generally need to notify the association before work starts in order to be accepted for cover.

If the work you are having carried out is covered by one of the guarantee schemes mentioned below, include their details in the contract.

Here we list some of the main schemes. See also the appendix of trade associations on page 153 for details of other insurance arrangements.

Building Guarantee Scheme (UK) Ltd*
Sponsored by the Construction Employers Federation, this covers customers in disputes about quality and also provides two and a half years' cover after the completion of jobs costing between £500 and £100,000.

Federation of Master Builders IBG
A Masterbond Warranty from a Federation of Master Builders member is a safe option. For 1.5 per cent of the total cost of the job,

it protects against defects due to faulty workmanship and materials for two years, and against structural defects for a further ten years. Contact FMB★ for further details.

Guarantee Protection Insurance Company (GPI)★
This is a guarantee scheme specifically for damp and timber treatments carried out by member firms of the British Wood Preserving and Damp-proofing Association (BWPDA)★. A one-off payment provides full cover for ten years for structural waterproofing or 20 years for remedial wood treatment, damp-proofing and wall ties. It is intended to cover customers if the original treatment firm is no longer in business.

Homepro★
Homepro offer a range of flexible IBGs, including guarantees of up to ten years, deposit indemnity, and a comprehensive IBG which is index-linked, so that the value of your work is protected against inflation.

Independent Warranty Association (IWA)★
Underwritten by Lloyds, the IWA has traditionally offered cover mainly on windows, conservatories, kitchens and bathrooms. It now also provides a ten-year IBG that does not exclude any components and will give protection in the event of a contractor going out of business. It ensures that any incomplete work is finished, and also that any necessary remedial work is done.

Joint Contracts Tribunal IBG
The Joint Contracts Tribunal★ allows for an IBG option on its Minor Works Contracts, which can provide cover for disputes about the quality of the work as well as against the insolvency of the contractor, on jobs ranging from £500 to £100,000.

Liability Insurance

According to the Association of British Insurers*, Liability Insurance pays for compensation when someone has been held legally liable for an adverse event – from a plasterer falling off a ladder to a roof falling in during a loft conversion. This type of insurance is generally required by businesses, not individuals, and comes in two main types.

Employers' Liability (EL) insurance is compulsory by law for nearly all employers, who must insure for a statutory minimum of £5 million, but in practice, most policies offer £10 million minimum cover. Employers' liability insures the employer against their legal liability for injury, disease or death to employees sustained by them and arising from their employment.

Public Liability Insurance (PLI) covers a business's legal liability to pay damages to members of the public for death, injury or damage to their property which occurs as a result of business activities. With the opportunities for accidents offered by the building trade, a builder without Public Liability Insurance is one to avoid.

PLI also covers the builder's legal fees and costs if he gets taken to court by you, the client. PLI for £1,000,000 may seem a lot, but sometimes single awards for injury can exceed that, and if there is a risk of, say, a spreading fire or multiple personal injuries, there could be several claimants competing for a piece of the compensation pie.

For more information on workplace compensation and employers' liability issues visit *www.abi.org*, or contact the Association of British Insurers* .

Chapter 3

Professional planning

General builders can tackle many jobs. However, for all but the simplest home improvement schemes, most people will appreciate the inside knowledge that experts can bring, especially when it comes to solving design problems, making the best use of existing space, and planning the best way of creating more of it. You will also need professional help for projects that involve structural alterations to the house to ensure that new foundations, walls, load-bearing lintels and the like are strong enough to do their job. On a major project, unless you have extensive experience of building work, you may want to hand over the entire management of the job to the professionals, letting them deal with everything from the early design stages to getting official permission, awarding contracts and supervising the work (see Chapter 5 for more on project management).

Architects

Architects must be registered with the Architects Registration Board★. Many architects are members of the Royal Institute of British Architects (RIBA)★, the Royal Incorporation of Architects in Scotland (RIAS)★, the Royal Society of Architects in Wales (RSAW)★, or the Royal Society of Ulster Architects (RSUA)★. You will find local architects listed in your *Yellow Pages* phone directory, and you can get the details of registered architects practising in your area from their professional bodies.

Just because someone is a registered architect does not mean that he or she will be the ideal person to deal with your building project, however. Some architects specialise in new building work or the commercial sector only, and it is important to establish early on whether the person you have approached is both experienced in relatively small-scale domestic work, and is genuinely interested in taking on the project. Personal recommendation is one of the best ways of finding someone suitable.

Once you have found someone, it is important from the outset to have a clear idea of what you expect your architect to do.

What your architect can do for you

The first step will be to hold a brief preliminary meeting, often free, at which you can outline what your project involves. Depending on the type of project, it can help to take along photographs of the house and any sketches and plans that you have drawn. It is also important to discuss at this stage what level of support you expect the architect to provide. The various stages involved in a typical building project include:

- preliminary project-planning advice
- preparing drawings to your specifications
- submitting plans for local authority approval
- obtaining tenders for the work from contractors
- preparing contracts
- preparing work schedules
- supervising site work
- issuing certificates for payment.

The more of these services you use, the higher the final bill. Depending on the extent of supervision required, the architect's fee may be charged as a percentage of the total cost of the job or, if little involvement beyond the planning stage is required, as a flat fee based on the amount of time spent on the work. Small, straightforward jobs are unlikely to warrant the considerable expense of employing an architect as your project manager (See Chapter 5).

Once you have agreed what you want done, how much involvement you expect, and what the fee will be, you should receive written confirmation of the relevant terms. If you do not, you should draw up a letter of appointment yourself, outlining exactly which duties you want performed.

Surveyors

Unlike architects, anyone can adopt the title of surveyor, and there are also several kinds of surveyor around, not all of whom are qualified in design and building work. You will need a build-ing surveyor, and, as with architects, you can find one by contact-ing the relevant professional bodies, such as the Royal Institution of Chartered Surveyors (RICS)★, for lists of their members in your area. Alternatively, look in the *Yellow Pages* under 'Surveyors – building', or rely on personal recommendation.

A building surveyor will carry out roughly the same range of duties as an architect, and a RICS member or similarly qualified surveyor will charge similar rates to those of a registered architect.

Consultants

Apart from architects and qualified building surveyors, there are also many firms and individuals offering to do similar work, but lacking any official registration. They may call themselves architec-tural consultants, architectural surveyors or architectural techni-cians – in fact, anything but architects. They do not have to adhere to any professionally monitored codes of conduct, and may not have professional indemnity insurance to protect you against losses resulting from negligent design or survey work. However, the work they do may well be of a first-class standard (or not), and they will certainly charge less than an architect or qualified building sur-veyor. If one is recommended to you, and has the references to back up the recommendation, by all means consider using them.

Local Building Control Officers

Many smaller-scale home improvement projects do not warrant the employment of an architect, surveyor or other professional adviser, but may need to meet the requirements of the Building Regulations in one way or another. This is where local authority Building Control Officers (BCOs) have a vital role to play.

BCOs are generally happy to give advice on what the Regulations require (as long as you do not overdo the questioning), and are aware that some helpful advice given while a building project is being planned can save both employer and contractor time and money later on if unacceptable plans or workmanship have to be rejected. They will also carry out site inspections, if appropriate, during the progress of projects not under the supervision of a qualified inspector such as an architect or building surveyor.

Specialist companies

There are several types of home improvement projects that lend themselves to the approach of the package dealer, including loft conversions, conservatories, and bathroom and kitchen refits.

Such companies offer to manage every step of the project, from initial design (often computer-aided) through to final completion, and this way of operating can seem very appealing if the alternative is to employ a range of professional advisers and separate contractors.

However, unless you take care to invite plans and costings from several such firms, and take the time to read the contract forms closely before you sign, you can find yourself at the mercy of the firm you have selected, without the back-up of any independent professional advice.

There are plenty of reputable firms with well-established businesses operating in this field. There are also numerous rogue operators, many of whom feature regularly in the consumer 'watchdog' horror stories of the press and television. As always, personal recommendation counts for a great deal, as can membership of a relevant trade organisation, such as the Federation of Master Builders (FMB)★, or the Glass and Glazing Federation★. You can get lists of member firms and help with complaints in two individual product areas: The Kitchen Bathroom Bedroom Specialists Association (KBSA)★ and the Conservatory Association★.

Chapter 4

Builders and other contractors

Although there are many different professions and trades working within the building industry, in practice, for small domestic jobs, the only person you are likely to be dealing with is the builder himself. Even on larger jobs involving many other tradesmen and officials such as the Building Control Officer (BCO), the builder is generally the man who stands between you and them, unless you opt to employ another professional as project manager (see Chapter 5). This chapter is about identifying some of the people who might temporarily occupy your house if you decide to go ahead with your building project.

General builders

If you call in the builders you may be dealing with a single individual, or several on larger-scale projects involving a number of different trades. Building firms may directly employ the different craftsmen they require, or else will subcontract the work to other firms as the need arises. Good subcontractors tend to work together, and a careful builder will have a reliable team of people to call on who know the ropes.

Single operators or small firms make up the vast majority of general builders, constituting roughly 50 per cent of the membership of the Federation of Master Builders (FMB)★ and, according to Department of Trade and Industry (DTI) estimates, 96 per cent of all construction firms in the UK. But builders are as different from one another as any other professional animal. There is no such thing as the average builder, but for most people employing a builder will mean dealing with a single operator – a man with a van or a lorry and a range of skills to suit most occasions.

A good general builder is like a good GP: multi-skilled and able to deal with most of the problems that walk through his door. His skills are acquired and honed throughout his working life, and possibly one of the most important attributes will be his bedside manner. Although in the building trade they are no substitute for actual construction-industry prowess, a pleasant demeanour and the ability to explain things clearly will help to build good relations with clients, and ensure things go as smoothly as possible during the course of the job. You should not employ someone if they are sullen and uncommunicative, or attempt to browbeat you.

General builders come from many different backgrounds. Some become builders after helping others and learning on the job, or after working on a project of their own, such as doing up a flat. Others follow a formal apprenticeship, then branch out on their own or with a partner. Formal qualifications are not particularly important – if you can follow architectural drawings then you can build a house. It can be a demanding job, requiring the builder to have a vast working knowledge of different trades and building laws. He must also be able to supervise the quality of subcontractors' work and deal with problems as they arise on site. Someone who has trained across many different areas will have a more thorough understanding of all the processes involved, and be able to tackle certain jobs such as carpentry, roofing or tiling himself.

In an unregulated industry, it may not be possible to tell where or how builders acquired their 'skills'. The construction apprenticeship system provided an enormous hinterland of experience for the working builder. It still exists today, but many young people are not prepared to put in several years on low wages in order to learn how to be a plumber, for example. A skills shortage has arisen – 72 per cent of FMB members reported difficulty obtaining skilled labour in the second quarter of 2003 – and the population of time-served builders has been gradually diluted by people drifting in from other professions. As older builders retire, it can be harder to find people who take a real pride in their work.

This has not always led to a lowering of standards, by any means, but it does mean that the man you are employing to reposition the load-bearing structures of your house may not have done it all that many times before. As with any profession, in general building you will find the incompetent and the super-efficient, the badly organised odd-jobber and the highly skilled, meticulous craftsman.

CASE HISTORY: Richard

Richard is a general builder who started at the age of 13, doing odd jobs for pocket money. He says: 'Dyslexic people like me tend to look for ways to communicate and express themselves through space rather than academia, and at its best this job gives you the chance to do that. I like to make homes that people want to go home to.'

During his varied experience of trades including painting and joinery, he has picked up valuable tips – such as learning not to cut corners after seeing other people being caught out. 'You can tell when something is being done right, and that's how I learned. Doing something properly is always the most economical way to do something. And you get a lot more job and customer satisfaction when you do it better than anyone else on the street.'

Most tradesmen are honourable, hard-working and handy to have around in a building-site situation. Unfortunately a substantial minority are irresponsible, something which greatly irks the straight-dealing, responsible majority who have to endure seeing their reputations slated in the media, and their profession viewed with almost the same distrust as that of journalists and politicians by the general public.

It is, however, possible to steer clear of shady characters who will rip you off. Later in this chapter we show how to be on the alert for the warning signs that a builder is not reputable, and how to find a reliable builder.

Building specialities

Whilst researching and preparing the launch of the Quality Mark scheme* (see page 157), the DTI drew up a list of 20 different skills which come under the heading of building trades. Many are often classed as specialities in their own right. It is not an absolute or definitive list, but it is a useful indicator of the kinds of task you might call upon a general builder to perform:

- general repair, maintenance and improvements
- masonry and blockwork
- carpentry and joinery
- pitched roofing
- flat roofing
- plastering
- damp-proofing
- insulation
- electrical work
- glazing
- painting and decorating
- tiling (wall)
- floor covering
- hardscaping and tarmacking
- underpinning
- foundations
- security (burglar alarm installations)
- heating
- fencing
- plumbing.

Which tasks a general builder will tackle himself, and which will be subcontracted out, will vary depending on the experience and abilities of the builder in question. Specialising in one trade – for example, gas fitting – is a lot more straightforward and predictable than general building work, with fewer surprises. People tend to take this route when they get older and want a reliable source of work which is less physically demanding.

Electricians

Electrical work is one area that many DIY enthusiasts prefer to leave to a professional. You may need an electrician either for a wholly electrical project, such as rewiring your house, or to carry out the electrical part of the work involved in another project. See page 98 for more detail about the electrician's role.

You can get the names of qualified electricians from the National Inspection Council for Electrical Installation Contracting (NICEIC)★, the Electrical Contractors' Association (ECA)★, and SELECT★. All three offer a complaints procedure and a completion-guarantee scheme.

Plumbers

Although small plumbing jobs are often tackled by general builders, it makes sense to employ a professional specialist for major projects, such as installing a central heating system, or plumbing in a new bathroom.

It is generally accepted that there is a shortage of qualified plumbers in the UK. The Construction Industry Training Board★ predicts that by 2007 an additional 29,000 will be needed. Most plumbers are able to pick and choose their jobs, so that if you have a cramped bathroom which needs converting, or a cracked lavatory pan on the fourth floor, you may find it difficult to get someone even to quote for it.

Also, because of the fairly unpredictable nature of plumbing – pipes can be corroded or oddly laid out, or not up to Building Regulation standards; fittings don't always fit, and leakages and accidents are always possible – the plumbing work on your job can become fractured and sporadic. The plumber might have to leave the site quite often for equipment or materials, and ultimately may begin working on other jobs to fill in time.

Plumbing rates vary significantly nationally, and are most expensive in the south of England. Try not to get charged by the hour.

Most plumbers also tackle central heating work, and may be members of the National Association of Plumbing, Heating and Mechanical Services Contractors★, or of the Heating and Ventilating Contractors' Association★. You can get the names of registered plumbers from the Institute of Plumbing★.

Always employ a qualified fitter – someone who is either registered with the Council for Registered Gas Installers (CORGI)*, or who works for British Gas* – if the work involves any work on your gas supply pipework.

Roofers

Roofing installation work is generally best left to the specialists because of the need to make the structure weatherproof as quickly as possible. Be wary of a one-man band who readily takes on roofing as well as other general building work. He might be OK, but he might be winging it.

You can get the names of registered roofers from the National Federation of Roofing Contractors★.

Specialist firms

If good general builders are like good general practitioners, with a range of skills able to meet a broad cross-section of consumer demands, then they will probably satisfy most of the people most of the time. But sometimes the service you require is more specific. Just as you wouldn't want your GP to be the one to take out your appendix (though no doubt he'd have a good go at it in an emergency), there are some building jobs which it is advisable to leave to specialist firms – see box below.

These projects contain idiosyncrasies which a general builder may have encountered only once or twice before in his working life, so he will inevitably end up spending time (and ultimately your money) solving problems. A specialist should have anticipated these difficulties and planned in advance around them. For the jobs described in the box below, you need a builder who is well-versed in the work involved – rather than one who spends his time on repair and maintenance.

Jobs best left to specialists

It is a good idea to employ a specialist firm for the following projects:

- conservatories
- extensions
- loft conversions
- conversion of a house into flats
- kitchen and bathroom refits.

Chapter 8 goes into more detail about the considerations you need to bear in mind when planning one of these projects, including applying for planning permission, dealing with problems, and what sort of expertise a specialist firm can contribute. For more on specialist companies see page 76.

Finding a specialist

There are a number of sources that you can use to find a specialist firm for a particular job. Magazine articles about home improvement will sometimes carry adverts for specialists in the type of work featured. Manufacturers or suppliers – of a bathroom, kitchen or conservatory, for example – should also be able to suggest suitable firms. There are also specialist trade associations, and organisations such as the Federation of Master Builders (FMB)* have builders and tradesmen who specialise in certain areas.

Finding a reliable builder

Finding the right builder is probably the most important single decision you can make when undertaking a project. A good builder will overcome the unforeseen obstacles and make the job a success, whereas an uninsured cowboy can potentially leave you broke and homeless. We explain here the best ways to ensure that you make the right choice.

Personal recommendation

The best way of finding a builder is by word of mouth, ideally by a recommendation from someone you know who is happy with work that has been done. If someone has done satisfactory work for friends or relatives, you can get a first-hand account of the person's workmanship, time-keeping, cleanliness and general attitude. You will also get the opportunity to inspect the work personally. This method may not, however, be viable if you have just moved to a different area, although asking for advice can be a good way of breaking the ice with your new neighbours.

If you can actually stand in someone's new extension and see that they are pleased with it, go with the firm that put it in – if they are available. It is often said in the building trade that you should never employ someone who can start right away, and there is an element of truth in this, because good builders tend to be recommended verbally from one job to the next and are booked up for months ahead.

If you are employing a professional adviser such as an architect, designer or structural engineer on your project (see Chapter 3), he or she may be able to recommend individual contractors. The advice should be completely impartial, but take up references anyway.

Spotting local talent

If a personal recommendation from a friend or professional is not possible, the next-best plan may be to visit building sites in your area. Skips, piles of sand and scaffolding all indicate builder activity, and people undergoing building work are usually happy to discuss their projects – unless, of course, they turned into disasters. Talk through the entire process with them and see if they would recommend the firm they are using. Ask if everything has gone according to plan, or whether they have hit any snags. For an overall flavour of what it is like, ask them, 'How has it been?' This may sound like a lot of trouble to go to when there are countless firms available through directories and on the Internet but, unfortunately, if you have to simply stick a pin in the local directory, the chances are quite high that you will end up with someone unreliable.

Many contractors put up a sign, or park their vans outside the house on which they are working, and will generally not mind being approached (although it is polite to make the initial contact through the householder). Alternatively, simply telephone the number displayed on the sign or van.

Trade associations and professional bodies

Many contractors in the home improvement sector belong to a trade organisation (and sometimes several), or are registered members of a professional body. These organisations can be a valuable source of local contacts; you can find a list of the main organisations in Appendix I at the back of this book.

Most trade associations have established procedures for negotiating complaints and protecting the rights of the customer, as well as measures for safeguarding the rights of the builder against unfair demands made by customers. Contact the relevant association to ensure that the builder's membership is current and there are no outstanding complaints registered. Always check more than one of the references given by your contractor and try, if possible, to visit the site to see an example of his work yourself and get the personal reassurance of someone who is satisfied.

If a firm or individual belongs to, or is registered with, a trade organisation, it may be a good indication of their professionalism, since many of these bodies require evidence of several years' trading and satisfactory accounts before granting membership.

Sadly, it has become increasingly common in recent years for unscrupulous contractors falsely to claim membership of trade bodies in order to enhance their image (see 'Be sure the logo measures up' on page 61). If you plan to contact a contractor via an advertisement in which any such membership is claimed, check the validity of the claim with the organisation concerned first.

You can get the names of building firms in your area from the Federation of Master Builders (FMB)★, the Building Employers Confederation★, or the Guild of Master Craftsmen★. The first two offer warranty schemes that guarantee materials and workmanship, and also completion of the work by another approved contractor if the firm you are using is unable to deliver for any reason.

Telephone directories

Your local *Yellow Pages* phone directory will list contractors under individual trade headings, and you will find plenty to choose from. Some have display advertisements giving details of the sort of work they undertake, and these may also reveal whether the individual or firm is a member of a relevant trade association, or has the necessary professional qualifications. Having a listing in a directory implies a certain level of permanence, although this does not guarantee performance standards.

The drawback to this method is that when you make contact, you are doing so 'cold', with little or no knowledge of whom you are calling. Start by asking whether they do the sort of work you require, and then ask them whether they would be prepared to put you in touch with satisfied customers in the area so that you can get a few references and also inspect their workmanship.

Local advertisements

You will also find contractors advertising in local newspapers and free sheets, and occasionally on newsagents' noticeboards. This is often a good way of finding individuals to carry out specific tasks, as well as general builders, but once again the contact is cold.

Individual contractors may be easier to contact in the evening or at weekends, although many of the more entrepreneurial types are never far from their mobile phones.

Cold-calling

You have probably already suffered from the approaches of telephone salesmen ringing out of the blue to ask whether you are interested in having your kitchen or bathroom refitted, your windows replaced, or a conservatory installed. By all means arrange a follow-up visit if you are interested in what they have to offer, but be on your guard.

Avoiding the cowboys

Trading Standards Officers and the Consumers' Association have repeatedly found that a sizable minority of the building trade regularly charge for work which they do not carry out, work to a poor standard, and/or carry out work that does not need doing. Prosecutions often follow such investigations.

According to the DTI, the poor workmanship of rogue tradespeople is now the major consumer problem in Britain: 106,000 complaints were registered with Trading Standards Officers in 2002. And although official complaints about cowboys are rising by about five per cent a year, the DTI believes that this represents the tip of the iceberg. They suspect that having spent large amounts of cash on a transaction, many people are simply too embarrassed to complain, instead paying out for bad workmanship to be remedied by another contractor. As public confidence in builders wavers, it is possible that the cowboys could be costing the industry £4 billion a year in lost profits and business.

Lifting the lid on poor practice

During an eight-month 'sting' operation by Surrey County Council in 2002, 72 separate tradesmen selected randomly from directories were called to a property to quote for a variety of problems. Twenty-one of them – 30 per cent – did not even bother to keep the

---

appointment. A quarter of those who did turn up demonstrated incompetence or attempted to defraud the council. Thirteen were under further investigation at the time of writing.

Be sure the logo measures up

In November 2002, *Which?* magazine interviewed more than 1,000 people. Seventy per cent said that they would be more confident using a builder who displayed a trade association logo, but the respondents' ability to recognise bona fide logos was not well honed. For instance, thirteen per cent of people claimed familiarity with the logo of The Society of Registered Builders – despite the fact that it was a fictitious invention created by designers from *Which?* – and seven per cent were convinced they had heard of the non-existent Association of Approved Garages. Both fake organisations were identified by more people than recognised the genuine logo of the National Federation of Roofing Contractors (NFRC)★.

The investigation also found that most people felt reassured by a logo on an advertisement, and believed that members of a trade association had to adhere to strict professional standards. However, less well known is that some associations do not vet would-be members, check members' work, offer complaints or arbitration procedures, or require members to be appropriately insured or indemnified against going out of business.

You should look for an organisation which is reasonably difficult, and expensive, to join, as this shows that contractors value their membership. Another good sign is if all complaints are registered (even if they are ultimately resolved amicably). Members are unlikely to cause trouble because they will not want to reflect badly on the association as a whole. In the case of minor disputes, just mentioning the association to which your builder belongs may be enough to bring him back on track. The better associations understand that it is good business practice to keep customers happy as well as to represent their members.

As mentioned above, always double-check with the trade association itself if a company carries a trade logo in its advertisements. Some cowboy outfits make false use of trade logos or may have been expelled after publication – don't assume that the publisher will have checked this.

CASE HISTORY: Derek, the bad-boy builder

Derek has spent most of his life in and out of the building trade – with occasional forays into used-car dealing, warehouse work, and Wormwood Scrubs. He is perpetually in the red, although he works in the black economy. He gets paid in cash – as much as he can get up front – and is way behind on his taxes. He is uninsured and he hasn't paid a National Insurance contribution in five years.

Derek advertises in the local directories with a crisp-looking, professionally produced advertisement which features the crests of several trade associations to which he does not belong. He leaves sites unattended for weeks and his jobs often end acrimoniously and/or unfinished, which has led to several county court judgments against him – though the difficulties of extracting recompense have meant that customers who complain are generally left unsatisfied.

Derek's strategy is to live off his cash advances and run as many jobs simultaneously as he can, which means a snarl-up in one in three or four of the jobs he takes on. He can just about do the work properly if he has to, but it never occurs to him to apply himself. Derek usually prefers the excavation part of the job to the reconstruction process, and begins to lose interest in the job once most of the destruction is complete.

He tells customers that he can get them a discount on materials, though his credit with local suppliers is so bad that he has to travel considerable distances in order to find outlets which know him insufficiently well to do business with him. This extra cost, plus another mark-up, is passed on to his hapless customers. Having paid over the odds for materials, Derek's customers often find that he has actually used whatever he happens to have in the back of his lorry at the time – he may use sharp sand and builder's sand interchangeably, so that his mortar is coarse and his concrete is weak. Coastal Dereks even use beach sand, gathered at night, charged to the client and seriously undermining the strength of the finished concrete.

Derek thinks nothing of knocking out a structural wall and leaving someone's house teetering on a single support prop while he goes off in his lorry to get more materials, stopping for lunch on the way back. All this counts as 'travel time', payable at his normal, exorbitant day rate. Because the customers have paid in cash to avoid VAT, and there is no written contract, Derek knows that he is in a strong position, and is not averse to using his considerable physical presence as a negotiating tool. As a result, most dissatisfied customers pay up and keep quiet, generally resorting to employing another builder to clear up Derek's mess.

Tips on what to look for

Distinguishing a good contractor from an indifferent one (or, indeed, an out-and-out rogue) is never easy. Below are some key points to bear in mind.

- A good general builder may be booked up by word of mouth for more than a year ahead, and will always be busy. It can be well worth waiting to get the best man for the job.
- Never employ anyone who comes round door to door – no decent builder has the time to do that. Good contractors often never advertise, because they get all the work they can handle through personal recommendations from one job to the next.
- It is a good idea to be flexible in your schedule to get the builder you want, rather than going for someone you are unsure about but who fits in with your exact timetable. The latter option could easily be a false economy.
- A serious builder should be prepared to see you at the planning stage in order to go through your project, explain what's involved, and maybe give you some ideas and a little guidance – even if you end up using someone else.
- Don't just go for the cheapest quote, because you will find that it gets more expensive as you go along and you are likely to encounter unforeseen add-ons. A good builder will warn you about the likelihood of things like damp being discovered and will build it into the quote, so that you don't get any nasty surprises.

Questions to ask yourself

Here are some useful pointers as to whether the individual or firm
you have contacted is likely to be competent and trustworthy.
Unsatisfactory answers to any of these questions suggest that you
might be wise to look elsewhere.

- When you first telephoned, did you get a clear and firm
  response to your inquiry? A positive 'yes' and the offer of an
  early appointment is a good sign. Indecision, or a promise to
  call back, is not.
- Was he punctual for the first appointment? (If he can't get it
  together to turn up now, what might he be like in the middle
  of the job?)
- Check out his van. This vital business tool should be clean, in
  good repair and ideally proudly displaying his business details
  on the side in clear lettering. If it is battered and anonymous it
  speaks volumes about the driver.
- Was he interested in what you wanted doing? Or was he just
  going through the motions and thinking about the cheque at the
  end? A good contractor should be ready with positive suggestions regarding alternative ways of doing the job, or different
  materials to use, while still leaving you to make the final decision.
- Did he offer – ideally without prompting – to provide references from satisfied customers? Be wary if he says he has just
  started work in the area.
- Did you like him as a person? If you employ him you'll be seeing a lot of him, so don't go for someone who gives you the
  creeps.

Inviting quotations

Once you have established their interest in the project, and perhaps had an initial site meeting with them, you should now write
to the builder or firm asking for a quotation for the work.
Approach at least three contractors in order to ensure that you get
the most competitive price, and make it clear to each that they are
in competition for the contract. Do this well in advance of the time
when you hope the work will start: good builders are usually
booked up for months in advance.

If the project is relatively straightforward – fitting replacement windows, for example, or installing a new bathroom suite and tiling the room – the contractor may be able to price the job simply by visiting your home. For more complex jobs he will need further information: proper drawings as well as detailed specifications that include any particular products that you want used. Your architect might be able to provide these, if you are using one. Make sure that you have enough copies for each contractor.

When you ask for a quotation, tell the contractor by when you want his response; it is usual to allow up to four weeks for this. Ask how long the quoted price will remain valid, and whether it includes VAT. The contractor must be registered for VAT if he is to add it to your bill, and with sizeable sums involved it pays to check his registration with your local VAT office; unscrupulous and unregistered firms have been known to add it to bills as an illegal way of making a further 17.5 per cent profit out of unsuspecting and gullible clients.

Assessing quotations

Study all the quotations carefully. You will mainly be interested in the price, and you may find that the difference between individual quotations is surprisingly wide. Do not assume that a very high quotation means that you will get a first-class job: it is sometimes the contractor's way of saying that he does not want the job, but he will do it if you are prepared to pay over the odds.

Be suspicious of an unusually low quotation. This may mean that the contractor will be using inferior materials, or will be subcontracting parts of the job to inexperienced and inexpensive workers. Without revealing the estimates given in the other quotations, ask him to justify his price, and check that he has fully understood the scope of the project. You should accept a very low quotation only if you are confident that you will get what you want for the price. You may, of course, get a bargain.

The amount of detail you receive will vary from firm to firm. The job should be broken down into individual stages (this breakdown is known as a schedule), and should clearly state where you have specified that particular materials or fittings are to be used. The schedule should also say who is responsible for supplying these items (see page 43) .

If you did not specify the individual items needed for the job – the bathroom suite, for example – the quotation will include them within what is known as a 'provisional sum'. This will be replaced in the final bill by the net cost of whatever the contractor fits, as well as a proportion of his overheads and profit charges. Where he will be employing specialist subcontractors for parts of the work, he should identify these parts, and should include a prime cost (pc) sum in the quotation, representing the subcontractor's own price for the work. Again, the main contractor will add his overheads and profit to this figure.

The quotation should also cover the following points.

- The person who is responsible for obtaining any necessary official permission before the work can get under way. If permission has already been obtained, the quotation should state that work will be carried out in accordance with the approved plans.
- The person responsible for insuring the work and materials while the contractor is working in your home. Professional contractors should have both employer's liability and public liability insurance; these cover them for damage to property, and for injuries to their employees and third parties (see page 45).
- How any variations to the original specification, as far as materials, methods, timing or costs are concerned, will be agreed between the two parties. These should always be made in writing.
- When the work will start, and when it is likely to be completed.
- An itemised breakdown of the cost of the work, including VAT if appropriate, and details of how payments are to be made. Most contractors prefer some form of staged payment, especially on major projects. It is unwise to agree to pay upfront for materials: a reputable builder will have good credit with his suppliers, and will not have to pay for materials immediately.
- Details of any guarantees offered, especially if these are backed by insurance, or a trade organisation's indemnity scheme (see page 44). These details will eventually form part of the contract. Some firms include them on a separate standard form of contract sent with the quotation; others may print them on the

back. Read them carefully, and discuss any terms you do not understand, or which seem to favour the contractor unfairly. It is too late to change them once you have signed the contract. (See Chapter 2, page 37.)

Avoid the cash trap

It may be tempting to pay in cash to avoid the VAT. However, steer clear of this solution. If you have a contract with your builder, paying cash to avoid VAT means that, although the document is still legally enforceable, if you try to enforce it you will risk being charged with conspiracy to defraud HM Customs and Excise.

Making a decision

Other factors apart from the price may sway you in favour of a particular contractor. One may be able to start earlier than the others, or to complete the work more quickly. He may simply have made a good impression during your dealings with him, or may have done work of an impressively high standard for other customers which he has invited you to inspect. The choice is yours.

When you have made up your mind, and have clarified any points of disagreement over detail, write and accept the chosen quotation. It is courteous to notify the unsuccessful applicants at the same time.

Chapter 5

Project management

This chapter looks at the most likely people you could employ to manage a major building project and assesses their strengths and weaknesses. It also covers what to bear in mind if you decide to take the job on yourself.

Appointing a project manager

If your building project is large, elaborate and lengthy, employing someone else to act for you can be just what you need to keep things running smoothly. If it is, make sure that you allow the project manager to do exactly that. The whole purpose of appointing one is that he should be a single point of contact between you and the works. If you see something you don't like, or don't understand, or would like clarifying, it is better to go through the manager rather than tackling the builders about it directly. There is an old saying which project managers apparently sometimes use to discourage clients from this practice: 'Don't keep a dog and then bark yourself'.

For most people the 'gold star' option is to employ an architect and have him manage the whole job from start to finish. Unfortunately this is also the gold bullion option in terms of expense, and isn't usually justified for something like a simple kitchen refit. On smaller jobs it makes sense to cut down on personnel and it would certainly not be time- or cost-effective to have a full-time project manager standing over a single builder, 'supervising' while he carried out straightforward tasks that he has done a hundred times before and could perform blindfolded. For smaller, single-builder jobs it is almost always best to let the builder manage the project, reporting to you with as much or as little detail on the daily running of the works as you see fit.

For larger jobs, if the architect option seems like a distant fantasy financially, the other professionals listed on pages 73-76 also make extremely good project managers – almost certainly much better than you.

Advantages of employing a project manager

In general, if you cannot or do not want to manage the project yourself, it is probably best to engage the professional who is most involved. If ground and timber conditions are likely to be an ongoing issue throughout the works, such as in an old barn restoration on a muddy hillside in Suffolk, perhaps the surveyor would be best placed to monitor the day to day running of the job.

If you are planning a Norman Foster style glass and aluminium addition to your central London Georgian townhouse, perhaps the structural engineer might have the most pertinent overview.

As jobs increase in size and complexity the benefits of hiring professional management also increase. There is a point at which it becomes foolhardy not to. Trying to tackle a three-storey extension project with no management or building skills would be courting disaster.

The Association for Project Management (APM)★ lists more than 50 core skills involved in managing a project successfully. As well as the obvious ones, like coming up with a detailed schedule, estimating resources, and managing the performance of a team, are more arcane areas such as risk management.

Risk management, to most people, might mean 'keeping an eye out for things that might go wrong', but to a trained project manager who has studied modules on risk management theory, it breaks down into clearly identifiable areas of risk:

- commercial or contractual
- product- or service-based
- legal
- political
- financial
- technological
- weather-related
- environmental
- 'acts of God'
- schedule-based
- entirely unplanned.

All these categories need to be anticipated, prepared for and thought about. That may sound like overkill on a simple kitchen extension, but each category contains what could be genuine risks for your project, and it can be advisable to have someone look out specifically for these factors. Other aspects of managing your project identified by the APM that you might want to delegate to someone else are:

- assessing the working methods of the team
- quality control, and
- providing feedback on performance.

Assessing the performance of people carrying out processes you have never seen before – and then providing meaningful, yet tactful, feedback to a builder standing in the ruins of your bathroom who thinks he's done a pretty good job so far in the circumstances – can be daunting. The trained project manager is equipped with a range of interpersonal skills, including counselling techniques – no doubt useful for dealing with builders who are oversensitive to criticism of their work.

Architects

Architects can have a reassuring presence on the site. They wear slightly different clothes from everyone else, and you know they have had to study for a long time (it takes them seven years to qualify). As project managers they seem perfectly placed. Having come up with the plans in the first place, it is a matter of professional pride for the architect to see them implemented according to his forecasts. And having an architect as the single point of contact makes sense because builders automatically defer to architects, whereas they may assume ignorance on the part of homeowners. Builders who might 'try it on' with you wouldn't even think about doing so with an architect.

This deference is not without good cause. The architect is a potentially lucrative client for the builder, who is likely to want to perform well in front of someone with the ability to provide him with future work. In addition, architects are highly knowledgeable across a wide range of areas, from environmental law to soil mechanics, aesthetics and energy conservation, as well as how to run a building site.

Although architects are the natural choice to lead most domestic building projects in which they are involved, their time is expensive. Most architects offer their design services separately but are likely to charge for project management services at a similar rate. Many people opt for using the architect's design skills and employ a cheaper – though no less proficient – manager from a less expensive profession.

But even if you pay for 'gold star' treatment from an architect, there is still scope for wide variability in the service provided. Before making a choice you should carry out the same sort of research that you would to find a reliable builder, such as following up word-of-mouth recommendations and checking references.

The case for appointing an architect

- An architect will know about building laws as well as matters such as drainage, water penetration and insulation. He will make sure that plans are passed by Building Control, so a job can start on time.
- An architect – especially one specialising in domestic work – may well have his own team (or teams) of builders whom he takes round from job to job. You are not obliged to use them, but it can make life a lot easier if you do.
- An architect will know how to draw up proper specifications for materials, and make sure that they are adhered to. Otherwise you could end up paying for a Mercedes-Benz level of fixtures, but end up with the equivalent of an old jalopy.
- Architects pay attention to detail. On one job involving a new integral garage and two outside gates for example, there would have been nine separate keys, but the architect coordinated them so that the owner had to carry only one.
- Architects are trained in aesthetics, and an architect-designed addition could enhance the value of your home.

CASE HISTORY: Using an architect

Les and Rowena used a structural engineer's drawings when they were planning to convert their loft into an artist's studio for Rowena to paint in. Originally they wanted to work directly with their builder, but they ended up appointing an architect when they decided that elements of the design were a bit 'clunky'. The architect enhanced the engineer's basic plan considerably, bringing in a lot more light and making far better use of the space. He also proved invaluable during the negotiations with the builder.

The job cost £30,000 and took three months. A payment schedule was agreed to release one-third of the funds at the end of each month. But by the end of the second month not all of the scheduled work had been done.

'The architect was very good and visited the site to assess the amount of work that had been done that month,' said Les. 'In the end he persuaded the builder that only £8,000 of work had been completed, and the builder accepted it with good grace. We were also very impressed with how the architect listened to our needs and then worked them into the design, for example widening the staircase so that Rowena could carry her materials up the stairs and bring her paintings down more easily. He also ensured that our contract with the builder specified that work took place only between 8 a.m. and 6 p.m., Monday to Friday, and that no materials or machinery were left on site, so we wouldn't be coming home to find a cement mixer on our lawn.'

The most reassuring part of having the architect handle the entire project was being able to have complete faith in the finished product. 'Knowing that it complied with all the regulations gave us peace of mind – he saw to all that,' said Les, 'and guaranteed that the roof wasn't going to leak. He insulated us from the whole process, and gave us exactly what we wanted.'

Surveyors

Surveyors have a fairly strong card to play in the project managerial stakes, in that a significant portion of their training is given over to project management and, more specifically, construction project management. The Royal Institution of Chartered Surveyors (RICS)* has a Project Management Faculty, which publishes its own newsletter. At a guess, the builder you were considering for the job probably does not subscribe to this, whereas a surveyor just might.

The case for appointing a surveyor

- Team coordination skills are part of a surveyor's training. Surveyors can also specialise in project management, at undergraduate and postgraduate level, in addition to their training in general surveying work.
- Surveyors have a tremendous amount of experience in anticipating problems, and they understand that there will be provisional problems which were not anticipated at the outset. For example, unforeseen timber conditions are one of the major problems that can slow a job down. And if there is evidence of dry rot in a timber, the consultant you want on site is a surveyor – someone who understands the problem and knows exactly what has to happen next.

Structural engineers

The good thing about a structural engineer is that he is a 'numbers man'. If his numbers don't add up, the building will fall down. The architect will defer to the engineer on matters of load bearing and what is structurally achievable, so will be able to accept an engineer as project manager (even if he dismisses this as a non-commissioned officer role).

Unfortunately, as well as cowboy builders, cowboy engineers also exist and are arguably an even bigger hazard. Astonishingly, anyone can call themselves a structural engineer and set up in practice, as long as they can get their drawings passed by Building Control – something which the Institution of Structural Engineers* regularly lobbies the government to legislate against. Ironically, the Institute's rigorous, seven-hour examination has been adopted by several other European countries as a means of regulating engineers, although this is not enforced in the UK. The letters MIStructE after an engineer's name indicate that five or six years after graduation, he has voluntarily subjected himself to this gruelling membership requirement in order to join the Institution. In 2002 the exam had a pass rate of 26 per cent. Look for someone with this qualification where possible.

The case for appointing a structural engineer

- Structural engineers know about risk. Right from the outset, they will be looking at what can go wrong: whether the age of the building means it won't withstand a conversion, or whether you can get the materials you need on site.
- Architects could be said to occupy the periphery of a job compared with a structural engineer, who may be working at his desk one minute and then be in the thick of things on site the next.
- A good structural engineer will have a working relationship with several reliable builders. As project manager he might recommend that certain trustworthy people are used – and this could make all the difference to the success of your project, because a lousy builder can cause a lot of problems.
- Architects excel at spatial planning. But a structural engineer understands materials more thoroughly, and will be able to anticipate time delays more effectively because he is more closely involved with the job.
- The builder may take a structural engineer more seriously than an architect because his role is more hands-on.

Builders

Chapter 4 explains the role of the general builder. Builders are well positioned to manage a project, because it is their project too. No matter who else is involved, from architect to structural engineer, the builder is still the principal player in any building programme. He is the one who actually sets the bricks in the mortar and secures the timbers and joists (or oversees the people who do), and generally operates at the sharp end of the construction process. If the builder doesn't do his job properly, then the project is in big trouble.

In addition, if you are fortunate enough to be able to employ a Chartered Builder for your project, he will be well qualified and will have explicit project management training, in accordance with the Chartered Institute of Building (CIOB)★ code of practice. The CIOB suggests that its members are well placed to act as 'independent client advisers', understanding users' needs and objectives. It suggests they should be engaged right at the start of the project to give impartial guidance on how to proceed.

A builder certainly understands the costs, the problems which can be caused by the interaction of all the contractors, and the range of other problems likely to arise. However, having a builder to manage the project could potentially result in a conflict of interests when it comes to explaining away delays, or negotiating more money for extra work owing to unforeseen circumstances.

The case for appointing a builder

- The builder shares the risk with the client. On a domestic job in particular, you are very much 'in it together' since it is a joint enterprise where you trust him with your house, but he also invests time and money and trusts you to pay him on time.
- The builder knows the job inside out, and what needs to happen, where and when, better than anyone.
- Part of a builder's job has always been people management and organisational skills. And a domestic-scale building project is not a hugely complicated management operation.

Specialist companies

Specialist companies, such as suppliers and fitters of kitchens or conservatories (see page 56), tend to be project-managed efficiently, though often down the end of a telephone. Generally the job is well planned in advance and carried out by extremely experienced fitters who have probably fitted the same kitchen into a similar building several times recently. Because of the need to maintain a good reputation and a high turnover, such firms tend to be very attuned to customer feedback.

Managing the project yourself

Unless your project belongs in the box on page 56, there is, of course, another person who could potentially manage the project: you. It seems temptingly easy at first. Materials will arrive, contractors will turn up, and the work will proceed until it is done, which is more or less how it does happen. More or less. However, the noise levels, the unpredictability, and the fact that it all takes place in your home can leave you feeling besieged and stressed out. Depending on how you feel about this, if you do take on the job it can be an extremely rewarding, exhilarating and worthwhile experience. And the outcome is something that will last for years.

Preparing for project management

A long-established strategy for approaching a construction project is to break the task into several stages, most of which are about planning.

- **Feasibility assessment** This is where the basic numbers are crunched. Can it be afforded? Is there a good business case for it? What are the risks? Skimping at this stage can leave serious questions unanswered.
- **Strategy development** This is the critical planning stage, at which the key personnel are selected and briefed interactively, so that their expertise is harnessed and applied to the planning of the project. Procurement strategies are specified, communication lines and the chain of command are established.
- **Preconstruction finalisation** You go through the plan one more time with all the key players.
- **Construction** The easy bit (if you are lucky).
- **Completion, handover and occupation** Bear in mind that residents and users will need time to get used to a new building or facilities. So go easy on yourself. Your whole organisation – cats, dogs, kids, goldfish, other dependants and spouse – may require an adjustment phase.

If you are planning, managing and running your own home improvement project, you can keep things going smoothly by paying the same attention to detail as a professional would throughout the job. Start by doing your homework thoroughly, researching the products and materials you intend to use, and the scope of the work involved.

Keep a project folder

In addition to having a copy of the contract (see Chapter 2), it is a good idea to keep a project folder, containing the following:

- a simple A4 description of the programme of events, delineating the sequence of events and timescale, photocopied, so that adjustments can be marked. (See 'Schedule of Works' in Chapter 2, page 43.)
- a sheet of A4 paper, blank apart from the title 'Agreed Changes Sheet' (don't think you won't be needing it). All changes should be agreed in writing – with costs too.
- line drawings and specifications.

Before work starts, talk the schedule through with the builder while you are both looking at the A4 job description, so that you can be absolutely sure that you are both 'singing from the same song-sheet', and then leave the folder somewhere conspicuous so that it can be accessed regularly throughout the job. Near the kettle is a good place, but ensure it is in a sufficiently protective folder to weather tea stains.

Protect planned work

Skill number 44 in the APM armoury (see page 70) is to 'promote and protect planned work'. This is not as paranoid as it sounds. There will be threats to the planned work from a wide range of sources, including threats to key personnel involved. In practice this can mean that you end up fielding calls from your plasterer's in-laws in order to keep him on site, or organising for rubble to be stored in builder's bags in the garden at short notice because the skip hasn't arrived. The manager must be prepared to do anything which has to be done to keep the project moving.

Unplanned work may also threaten to interfere with your schedule. A late decision to put a shed in the garden which requires a concrete base may monopolise the cement mixer and key personnel to the detriment of planned work. Be sure that enthusiasm for extra-curricular projects does not impede progress towards the originally specified goals.

Financial management

This is a crucial element of control and it must be handled properly. Your agreement or contract (see Chapter 2) should specify the payments schedule, which often involves staged payments, released weekly or monthly or at certain key milestones of the job. Be sure that these milestones have actually been reached and the agreed amount of work has been completed before parting with funds. The simple rule is: never pay up front for work that hasn't been done. Small builders tend to operate with tight cash flows, so it is normal to release sufficient funds for materials, and then regularly throughout the job as work is completed.

Subcontractors

If a professional is employed to manage, he takes care of the subcontractors through an account in his name, or funds forwarded on request. If you are managing, they should be briefed and paid in the same way as the builder, with time-staggered payments as necessary.

If you are acting as project manager you should be introduced to every subcontractor working on the site and should ensure that they are briefed to the same degree of detail that you specified with the builder. Transmission errors in the chain of communication are now your responsibility. In particular, if you have any special or unusual requirements, such as heavier-than-average wrought-iron lamp fittings, it is best to talk through them directly yourself with the subcontractor to make sure he knows.

If, as often happens when work gets under way, you decide that you would like a subcontractor to carry out some extra work, do not instruct him yourself, because this work will fall outside any existing contract, which can lead to messy disputes about cost. If it has definitely not been specified in the original contract, ask the main contractor to give you a price for it (then enter it in the log and on the Agreed Changes Sheet).

The tea rota

Just because you're 'the Guv'nor' doesn't mean that you can miss your turn in the tea rota. It means, if anything, that you have to take it more seriously.

CASE HISTORY: Henry

Henry has employed builders for 20 years, and believes that mastering the tea ceremony is among the most important aspects of managing the job.

'Get the tea-making right and the rest will follow,' he says. 'Get to know what everybody likes to drink – tea with three sugars, black coffee, whatever it is – and make sure that it's there for them just as they like it at the appropriate times.'

The importance of the ritual of tea drinking cannot be underestimated on a building site, he feels. 'On our latest job of converting a pair of flats back into a single dwelling, for some of the time the whole site was without proper washing-up facilities, so we bought paper cups for the builders,' Henry says.

'Benedict, our four-year-old, liked the builders to have their names on their cups, so each morning I would write their names on to a cup with one of Benedict's crayons, and he would draw a picture on the cup to show what each man did. So the bricklayer had a little trowel, the electrician had a bolt of lightning, and so on. It stopped the cups getting mixed up, but we found that it also cut down on waste, too, because the builders became attached to their cups and held on to the same one throughout the day.'

Chapter 6

Ensuring the job goes smoothly

All building work is disruptive. The degree to which it will interfere with your everyday life depends on the scale of the project and how it is being supervised. In an ideal world, you would employ an architect or surveyor to manage the entire project, and then go away on holiday until it was finished. In reality, however, you will simply have to live through it.

The secret of making life bearable during the upheaval lies in having a complete understanding of what the job will involve, and in making thorough preparations before work starts. Chapter 7 outlines the main stages of a large-scale building project, and Chapter 8 provides further details of specific jobs. Here we give some general suggestions on making preparations. Not all will apply to every project, but by checking them off one by one you will be able to decide which are relevant to you.

Before work starts

One of the most important steps to take before work starts is to inform your neighbours of what you are planning to do. They will already have been notified by your local authority about any large-scale projects requiring planning permission, but even if they have no objections in principle to the work being carried out, they may well react with horror once it starts. If you have them on your side from the beginning, life will be much easier for all parties. Sort out the following issues in particular.

- In semi-detached or terraced properties, work may affect party walls. Construction work on such structures is covered by the

1996 Party Wall Act. Before work starts it is best to call in a surveyor to carry out an inspection of both sides of the wall (which will obviously require your neighbour's consent), and make written notes as to its condition, which both parties should then sign and date.

- Your contractors may need access from your neighbour's property – for example, in order to erect or dismantle scaffolding. You cannot proceed without the neighbour's permission, so make sure that this is forthcoming, ideally in the form of a letter.
- Dust, and possibly larger pieces of debris, will inevitably fall on your neighbour's property as the work proceeds. Tell your neighbour that you will clean his or her windows, wash down paintwork, sweep paths, and so on, whenever necessary, and that your contractor is insured for any damage that he might cause to the property or to any vehicles parked on it.
- Building work is bound to be noisy. Try to agree with your neighbour the times when particularly noisy work will cause the least disruption.

As far as preparing your own house is concerned, here are some possible courses of action to consider.

- In areas of the house which are likely to be affected by the work, pack away all breakable items, and buy or hire dustsheets with which to cover your furniture and floor coverings (or remove them completely from the area if this is preferable and you have storage space available).
- Consider sending children or elderly relatives to stay with family or friends for the duration of the project if major disruption to the house and its services is anticipated. Arrange for your pets to go to boarding kennels, or to be looked after by neighbours or friends.
- Work out where you are going to store the materials for the project (whether in the open or under cover), and make sure that you have enough space available. It may be worth considering parking your car off the property, or at least well out of possible harm's way.

Dealing with contractors

When you are employing builders, you have every right to set the terms under which they will work in your home. You clearly cannot expect them to change into carpet slippers every time they cross the threshold, but you should make the ground rules clear from the start. Discuss with the builder in advance what working space, storage and access are needed to do the job.

Clearing the way

Begin by deciding on the builders' best access route into, or through, the house. Remove as much furniture as possible from this path, and ask your contractor to put down dustsheets along the whole route, taped or stapled so that they will not get scuffed up in use. It is a wise precaution to request them to lay heavy-duty plastic runners, so that wet or muddy boots do not mark your floor coverings through the dustsheets. It may also be worth taping protective packing material to any door frames through which tools and materials will have to pass. Insist that internal doors are kept shut whenever possible to prevent dust spreading right through the house, and use dustsheets to minimise contagion.

Keeping it clean

If builders have to trek into your area for any reason, then it is not unreasonable to insist that muddy shoes are left on the other side of the plastic. There is a lot of dirt out there; trips to the skip, for instance, inevitably involve spillage en route and dirt from outside being brought back in. It takes only a few careless trips from that environment into your screened-off area before it, too, starts to become absorbed into the site.

The enormous amounts of dirt that are generated by things like walls coming down will present a challenge to your dustsheeting regime, which needs to be maintained vigilantly if it is to survive. If work is going on downstairs, for instance, and the upstairs is being used only for storage and living accommodation, try to seal off the boundary completely using plastic or heavy cotton sheeting taped to the walls. If you have to surrender the stairs, seal yourself in on the other side as best you can, breaking the seal each time to pass through. A strip of gaffer tape (black plastic-coated cloth tape) refreshes the join when it no longer sticks.

As the work proceeds, you will have to be meticulous about clearing the decks as far as is possible at the end of each session if you are to avoid turning the whole house into a building site. Ask for paths and other access areas to be swept at the end of each working day in order to minimise the transfer of sand, cement and mud into the house.

Make sure that boarded runways are laid across lawns and flower beds to protect them from wheelbarrow tyres, and that special care is taken not to damage plants and shrubs. Insist that the contractor's vehicles are parked in the road rather than on your driveway, for spillages of oil and other materials could make a permanent mess.

Time spent maintaining tidiness and cleaning up will actually increase efficiency, because people will be able to move about the site more easily and identify what work needs to be done and what has already been accomplished. Clean working conditions also improve morale and raise working standards. Tidiness is also a health and safety issue: rubble, trailing flexes and discarded tools can present a serious hazard.

Providing facilities

The builder is under an obligation to provide welfare facilities for his staff. These should, ideally, be available to the builders on site so they do not have to enter your house.

Discuss which facilities the workmen may use, especially during lunch and tea breaks. You may be prepared to let them into your kitchen, or you may prefer to set up an old table and chairs in the garage or garden shed for their use; they may even prefer to take breaks in their van. If you are providing the catering facilities, make sure that they have access to the water supply and a kettle. Look out some cheap mugs, spoons and a tin tray, and leave tea, coffee, milk and sugar visible, so that they do not have to search the kitchen for these items. Provide ashtrays if they smoke, but make it clear if you do not want smoking inside.

If you have a downstairs cloakroom, allocate that for their use, put down dustsheets, and provide a good supply of old towels. Otherwise, unless you are prepared to let them use the family bathroom, it may be preferable to hire a chemical toilet and site it in the garage or garden shed for the duration of the project. Decide whether to allow them the use of your telephone; many contractors now have mobile phones, but may still expect to make outgoing calls at your expense. You can have such calls barred at the telephone exchange if you will be away from the house during the progress of the work.

Deliveries and materials

Make sure that deliveries to the site will not cause an obstruction, especially if they are to be left in the road. You need permission from your local authority highways department to do this, and also to park a skip in the road. Establish in advance who will be responsible for obtaining the necessary permits.

Remember that any obstructions in the road such as skips must be properly lit at night. Keep skips covered with a tied-on tarpaulin in order to stop other people dumping things in it. If piles of materials are to be left out in the open, make sure that they are put out of sight and well away from the road, so that unscrupulous passers-by are not tempted to help themselves.

Storage and security

Find out whether the contractors expect to leave their tools and equipment on the site at the end of the day. It is reasonable to allow builders to store their tools on site as long as the site itself is secure, so that the tools do not provide a temptation for intruders to enter. The builders should ensure that the tools are properly tidied away at the end of the day and boxed up where appropriate. You could offer to store larger items in your garage or shed, but you may prefer to ask them to take their tools home with them.

Make sure that any ladders are not a security risk, and that any windows that are accessible from ladders or scaffolding are secure. Above all, keep children and animals away from the work site for safety's sake.

If you will be at work or away while the job is being carried out, appoint one of the contractors 'head of security' and issue him with a set of keys. Make sure he knows how to lock up (and how to set and disarm the burglar alarm if you have one). Remove valuables from open display as a precautionary measure.

Safety

According to the Health and Safety Executive (HSE), construction is officially Britain's most dangerous industry. One hundred and six building workers were killed at work between 2000 and 2001, an average of two a week. Although most of these casualties occur on larger commercial jobs, the domestic site is not without serious hazards. Falling – or having something fall on to you – is the most common cause of death or injury on a building site, and falls can happen, for example, from scaffolding, or from a stepladder on to tools left lying around.

As well as tripping over extension leads and treading on nails, building sites present a great gamut of hazards, particularly for people who are unused to moving about on them. If you are going to be mingling with the builders on site, you will need to tiptoe around for quite a while before you learn the ropes.

As a general guide on how to move around on a building site:

- always take notice of what other people are doing and where their tools are, and try to anticipate what they will be likely to do next
- don't carry heavy objects above where people are working
- think about swinging ends: lengths of wood and pipe, and ladders, are slapstick waiting to happen, but going into casualty isn't actually that funny
- avoid collisions. Even the smallest accidental nudge when someone is carrying something heavy or awkward, or absorbed in fine work, can be catastrophic.

It is the builder's responsibility to train and provide all operatives on site with health and safety information, and to ensure that all plant and equipment are safe to use. If you see anything that contravenes this – a subcontractor not being issued with a protective breathing mask while laying roofing insulation, for example, or someone using a hammer with a wobbly head that is about to fly off – you should raise the matter with the builder and insist that he complies with guidelines.

The legal requirements for health and safety applicable to building work are laid out in legislation such as the Health and Safety at Work Act. You can find out more in the Building Regulation documents (see page 30), or look up the website of the Health & Safety Executive at *www.hse.gov.uk*.

What to wear on site

With heavy work going on, the affected area can legitimately be called a building site and, if you are project managing the job or even just visiting frequently, you should wear comfortable, loose, old clothes which you don't mind getting pretty dirty and possibly torn. Gloves are usually necessary only when lifting something specific. Steel toe-capped boots are not essential, though they are not a bad idea; apart from protecting your feet, 'steelies' can be very useful for levering heavy objects around in the event that you have to step in (if there is an absence of labour, for example). Wear thick-soled shoes at the very least, as abandoned architraves, carpet-edging and other offcuts will, even on the tidiest sites, inevitably find their way on to the floor. Watch out for nails sticking out of pieces of wood such as upturned floorboards: many shoes offer no protection against injury from protruding pieces of metal.

Supervising progress

If you are employing an architect, surveyor or other professional to supervise the project for you (see Chapter 5), he will visit the site at regular intervals, and will handle all the necessary communication with the contractors. This need not prevent you from taking an interest in how the work is progressing, but remember that you should pass any comments or complaints you may have to your supervisor, rather than making them directly to the contractors.

Managing the project yourself

If you are supervising the job yourself (see page 77), your main priority while work is under way is to ensure that the job is carried out according to the specification and the contract. Do not get too involved in the day-to-day running of the project: you will only get in the way and annoy the workmen, who generally hate being watched while they ply their trade. Intervene immediately only if you see something that is in obvious breach of the contract, and raise the subject tactfully rather than losing your temper.

Otherwise, simply check the progress made each evening, and, if you find anything amiss, either telephone the contractor there and then, or leave written instructions for him to read the next morning. On long-running projects it is a good idea to suggest a regular meeting – say once a week – at which progress can be discussed and any problems ironed out. If you are not at home during the day, make sure that you leave details of where you can be contacted if necessary.

Captain's log

As skipper of the vessel, it is a good idea to keep a log. A simple project diary, recording the key events of each day, can prove invaluable later on when disputes arise. Note when materials arrived, when the Building Control Officer visited, and when the electrician admitted that he was responsible for dropping his pliers in the bath and chipping the enamel. A note of which personnel are on site and the prevailing weather conditions will also prove a useful *aide-mémoire* for later on.

Mark here, too, any changes to decisions about specification which are agreed. The siting (and number) of plug sockets and light switches is fairly flexible and can be agreed and changed without too much trouble if they are mentioned in time, but having to use different tiles from the ones agreed, for instance, may make a big difference to your enjoyment of the finished work. Similarly, logistical difficulties with your preferred plumbing configuration sometimes threaten to reshape your bathroom or kitchen in ways you hadn't intended. In general if something has been agreed to be feasible in advance then it probably is, but if contractors can see a shortcut to an easier way they may press for the easier option. If they can argue that your idea can only be implemented if they charge extra for unforeseen circumstances, then you may want to compromise.

Changes will need to be agreed verbally with the builder as events unfold, and ideally noted in the log, as well as on your Agreed Changes Sheet. The log need not be up to Samuel Pepys' standard:

Weds 7 March, AM: Weather fine, materials arrived, no one on site all day.
Thur 8 March, AM: Weather sunny, work on drainage channels begun. Plumber not on site.

PM: Rain, excavation work inside.

Fri 9 March, AM: Weather good, skip arrived. Floorboards up in the lounge for electrics. Excavation inside continued. Extra light fitting in bathroom agreed.

PM: Plumber popped in but left for the plumber's merchants and did not return.

The advantage of keeping a record is that if at the end of the month the builder is behind, but wants his full monthly instalment and is arguing that the delays were unavoidable due to rain, or the plumber wants to charge you for half a day's work for 'that other Friday', you have something to go on.

Quality control

Ongoing monitoring of quality can be difficult when you have no experience of what you are dealing with, and the builder is your only adviser. Regular contact with the Building Control Officer will provide guidance on structural matters, but it is up to you to check that the final job meets all your specifications.

Keep track of changes

It's easy to lose all perspective in the middle of a building programme. Days and even weeks seem to merge into one another and little seems to have been achieved – apart from more, seemingly irreversible, damage to your house. And if you have witnessed some of the setbacks which have caused delays, it is easy to sympathise with the builder and allow deadlines to slide. But it is important to remain firm, negotiate any alterations to the deadline formally, and then make a note of the new arrangements in writing – in your log and preferably on the wall.

Chapter 7

The sequence of events

So the big day has finally arrived; you have followed the seven-point plan (see page 10), you are standing in a room which is stripped to the floorboards and waiting for work to commence, and the kettle is on. Obviously individual jobs vary enormously, but most large-scale building projects go through the recognisable phases outlined below.

Demolition, stripping out and excavation

First comes the excavation work, which may include digging outside to lay or alter foundations or drains. This is hard and time-consuming manual labour, and may involve placing large quantities of ready-mixed concrete.

The demolition and stripping out processes can be exhilarating and exciting, as things which you may have been using only yesterday, like kitchen cabinets or fitted wardrobes, are rapidly reduced to rubble and taken out to the skip. This should always be done with the minimum of force, unscrewing fittings where possible and using crowbars and bludgeoning implements only as a last resort, as they tend to inflict more damage than is necessary on the fabric of the building. As they are stripped of their usual clutter, rooms start to seem larger and lighter, and often they actually are, as partition and structural walls are moved around and excavated.

Any loose material, such as plaster or render in poor condition, unwanted tiles, sagging ceilings, polystyrene ceiling tiles, damp flooring in the basement, or partition or structural walls – in short, anything which is coming out – will be removed now. Channels will be dug into the walls for wiring and cables, which often causes more damage than anticipated or reveals further work that needs doing, such as more extensive replastering or the replacement of timbers degraded through rot.

After a few days of acclimatisation the euphoria passes and you begin to adjust to living in battlefield conditions. Normal supply lines are interrupted, there is a great deal of noise and dirt, and the sporadic rat-tat-tat-tat of power tools and hammers fills the air. Bulletins of wholly unexpected and potentially disastrous news arrive, but are averted by equally improbable events – the ceramic drainpipes have arrived cracked, but it's OK because a new set is on the way and they don't need to be laid today anyway, since the Building Control Officer (BCO) can't check the trench because he's got a bad back. After some quick reorganising disaster is averted, though inevitably the schedule slips back a couple of notches on its ratchet.

The skip cycle begins

Hiring a skip that will be sited on a public highway usually requires applying to the local council for a licence, which costs in the region of £25 per month. You do not need a licence if the skip is on a drive or private road. The skip itself is the ubiquitous end-point for all unwanted matter on a building site: rubble from walls coming down, earth from excavations, tea bags from what is left of your kitchen.

Often wheelbarrows are used to transport the debris along ramps made from scaffold boards or doors, but sometimes, if there isn't enough space, builder's bags are used. Builder's bags are heavy-duty rubbish sacks which can survive several journeys to the skip. They are less obtrusive than a wheelbarrow and become used as site-bins wherever there is dirty work. Offcuts of wood and plasterboard, broken bricks and tiles and general rubble should all be put into builder's bags and taken outside to the skip, not tidied into the chimney breast or under the floorboards. Casual conversations and unofficial breaks often take place by the skip, a bit like at the water cooler in an office, and the removal of a laden skip is certainly worth stopping work to behold at least once. The huge skip lorry usually leaves an empty one behind and the inexorable process of filling it begins again. Make sure that the skip lorry has somewhere solid to put down its jacking points; they can play havoc with an asphalt drive or a water company stopvalve cover.

Walls down

Any walls which are to come down will be stripped of their skirting boards and architraves, and services supplied to them will be sealed, disconnected or taken out. Acrow props (adjustable steel supports) will be braced against the scaffold boards placed at right angles across the joists in the ceiling and floor around the affected wall, and tightened up to take as much of the weight carried by the wall as possible. If a rolled steel joist (RSJ, or simply 'steel'), is going in, then it needs to be ready and nearby. This can be a nerve-racking experience, but it is a good idea to watch it go in if you can. If the walls and floors above are not supported by temporary props or if the beam is not packed in properly, there may be some slight movement in the house, and a crack is likely to appear somewhere in the fabric of the building as a result. This is like open-chest surgery for your house, and it does feel as though you are witnessing a major operation. With the RSJ(s) in place, the house will be utterly transformed into a spacious bomb site which bears no relation to how you remember your home, or how you imagine it will be in the future. Don't worry. This is normal.

Drainage

Drainage is covered by detailed Building Regulations. If you are laying new drains anywhere the BCO may want to inspect the works. He may specify the type of trench to be dug, the precise materials to be used and the exact way they should be laid to allow for local soil conditions. The Regulations specify precise angles of descent for the different kinds of pipes, bedding and surrounds, and careful notice should be taken of these. Builders and plumbers who are members of the Institute of Plumbing* self-certification scheme can self-certify minor internal and external drainage work of the sort that might be carried out on a typical kitchen or bathroom refit.

All the dirty water from your house is ultimately collected into one large pipe connected underground to the public drains, but there are three different kinds of dirty water which will find their way into your drains:

- waste water is from washing in sinks, baths and showers
- soil water is the discharge from WCs
- rainwater comes off the roof and the ground.

The precise gradient of each kind of pipe is specified according to its diameter, length and function. Sometimes angled joints are used; a 92½-degree elbow to join a vertical waste pipe to a horizontal one, for instance, ensures that the horizontal waste pipe falls away at the requisite tilt.

The water test

Before signing off the drains the BCO may carry out an air or water test. Stoppers are used to block off the ends of the drain, and air or water is pumped into it to see how it withstands the pressure.

Tests may not always be necessary as BCOs can use their discretion, but if one has been ordered then do not allow the trench to be filled in before the test has been successfully signed off, because if the drain fails there are few things more demoralising than digging out a trench you have just filled in.

Manholes

Manholes – or more correctly, inspection chambers – are for looking at the drains, and are usually found where a connection is made to the drain, or where drains intersect or change direction or gradient. They are also useful for diagnosing which part of the drain may be blocked, and for accessing the blockage with drain rods. If you lift a manhole cover, you may see two or more branches of drain converging, often consisting of half-channels of clay pipe set into steeply sloped concrete, though modern inspection chambers are cylindrical all-plastic affairs with a neat round cover. The precise layout of your drains can usually be ascertained by pouring water down individual sinks, baths and WCs and seeing from which branch, in which inspection chamber, it emerges. Your local authority may also have diagrams of your drains, which they may charge you to look at.

If you are extending your property over an existing manhole, Building Control will want to know all about it and might suggest leaving the existing inspection chamber operational, though double-sealed with a bolt-down cover, underneath your new floor. It can also be more permanently sealed, but either way another inspection chamber beyond the walls of the new building will need to be built, inspected and signed off by Building Control.

If there are several changes in direction in your drains (which should be avoided if possible), you might get away with rodding points at some of them, instead of the full inspection chamber. A rodding point is a branch in the drain which comes out more or less vertically upwards to the surface, where it is usually capped off with a screw-top cover for easy drain-rod deployment.

Soakaways
Increasing your roof space, building a patio, altering your driveway or changing your drainage in any way may result in the need for a soakaway. A soakaway is somewhere where excess rainwater can run off without going into the drain, but where it won't cause flooding. Some houses have all their rainwater disposal dealt with in this way rather than by surface drains, depending on soil conditions and ground water levels, and they are being encouraged on new developments.

A soakaway is basically a hole in the ground (the precise size of which has been specified by Building Control), filled up with hardcore, then sealed with a waterproof membrane and topped off with soil. Sometimes it needs an inspection chamber. A soakaway is a simple thing, but building one creates a lot of digging up and transportation of dirt, often through the house.

Cesspools
Cesspools are reservoirs of sewage stored in the ground until the water authority's contractor comes to take it away. They are more common in the countryside than in urban areas. Unless you are dramatically increasing the occupancy of the household and expected levels of waste generated, you shouldn't have to interfere with a cesspool when carrying out building work. Sometimes repointing may be necessary, and periodically sections of the chamber may need to be rebuilt. The contractor who calls to empty the cesspool may quote for this work, but it may not necessarily be the cheapest option.

Septic tanks
Similarly, don't interfere with a septic tank unless you have to (these also feature more in rural areas). A septic tank has its own delicate microbiological ecosystem which filters all domestic waste water from the house and allows it to soak away harmlessly into the soil. Bleaches, disinfectants and detergents will destroy the active bacteria

and result in the system breaking down and flooding. Enlarging it is a big job, which should be undertaken only if absolutely necessary, though the tank should be de-sludged every 12 months.

Structural work

The laying of foundations and the building of walls and supporting piers may also be going on during the demolition stage: all are heavy-duty and skilled processes to which it is difficult for you to contribute anything other than keeping out of the way. However, it is a good idea to keep an eye on the basic layout of the new walls as they are marked out, even at the very early bricklaying stage. It is not unheard of (though not popular with builders) for designs to change slightly at this stage – subject to architectural and/or Building Control approval, of course. If something is turning out radically different from how you imagined it, it may still be possible to alter the final layout. Sometimes partitions are moved when it becomes clear that the dimensions are impracticable; en-suite bathrooms are notoriously scaled down into shower rooms when it becomes clear that there either won't be enough space for the bath, or the bed.

Scaffolding

Scaffolding is necessary for two-storey extensions or roofing work to ensure safe working. For the householder it can become a bit like living behind bars, as the security implications mean that you have to be hyper-vigilant about keeping windows locked. If you have scaffolding outside, now might be a good time to invest in some extra security locks for your upstairs windows, because walking into your bedroom suddenly becomes as easy as climbing up a ladder from the street. It can also be a draw for children. Particularly with larger projects, scaffolding can speed up the job considerably, giving builders, building inspectors and finally decorators unparalleled access to areas in which it might otherwise be precarious to operate. Sometimes it allows them to move around the site without passing through the house, which is well worth the noise and inconvenience of having it erected. At the end of the day, the builder should make access to scaffolding difficult by removing ladders or fixing a scaffold board over the rungs of the ladder. See page 85 for more tips on security.

While you have scaffolding in place, it may well be worth thinking about what other jobs could be done where access is difficult. Exterior painting and re-pointing come to mind – both much easier done from scaffolding than from a ladder.

Concrete floors

If you are extending into the garden, or developing a basement, the builders will probably be laying concrete floors. These require a high degree of logistical organisation and coordinated teamwork, from the arrival of the materials to the bulk mixing of concrete and its delivery to the site of the new floor at the appropriate rate. If your needs are enormous, you may require a cement lorry booked to deliver the appropriate quantities of wet concrete at a particular time. This will entail organising parking permits, the purchase or hire of plastic storage tanks, and/or buying extra wheelbarrows to facilitate the timely distribution of a large amount of rapidly setting substance – beware, logistical mistakes can be costly.

However, most domestic concreting requirements can be met with a few cubic yards of sand and aggregate, some bags of Portland cement, and a dedicated labourer mixing up with a cement mixer and ferrying the wet stuff in a wheelbarrow to a man with a plank at the other end. The plank is used to ensure the even distribution of the artificial lake of concrete which gradually arrives and sets, like lava, to a degree of hardness which makes it inconvenient to alter. It is amazing what a two-man team can achieve in a day with this simple configuration. Whole areas which were recently bare earth are reclaimed for civilisation, over a waterproof membrane and with the occasional unobstructed duct for drainage and wiring poking out. Within a couple of days, the lava lake is frozen and ready to walk and build on.

The first fix

This is the first wave of trades being carried out by people who mean well, but still don't appear to be improving the quality of your life. The framework for the basic services is being laid, though it will be a long time before you feel the benefit of them. In order to accommodate cables and pipes, large holes have been made in the walls, perhaps revealing further work that needs to be addressed. This could include more replastering than was originally calculated, adverse timber conditions, dry rot, damp, and possibly even structural problems, such as foundations which are not as deep as they should be for the proposed works and which will require underpinning. This is normal and the builder should have anticipated any problems.

This might be a good time to talk to the builder about contingency plans. Unforeseen problems can have both predictable and unpredictable consequences. A new timescale could mean that your contractor will be running up against other jobs, and his availability is diminished. You could even be looking for a different contractor, depending on the scale of the problem. This is a worst-case scenario, of course, and the likelihood is that you will merely have encountered a few unforeseen problems, slipped a little behind schedule, and had to find a bit of extra money.

Carpenters

Carpenters – known as 'chippies' – arrive like heroes riding into the breach, bearing positive-looking lengths of sawn or planed wood, erecting things which begin to bring order to the space. They build stud walls, often leaving them open-sided so that pipes and cables can be laid inside. Carpenters also build floors and staircases, they fit joists, and make hatchways and door frames; during the second fix they do boxing in, make bespoke shelving, and fit kitchens and worktops (see page 102) – all positive and necessary developments which are easy to understand and offer visible benefits. Carpenters are usually precise and relatively clean workers compared with some other trades, particularly when compared with the excavation process which has gone before. But, just as you are warming to your carpenter, he is gone. There is only so much he can do before the next in the succession of trades arrives: the electrician, and possibly even the plumber.

Electrical wiring

Throughout the first fix the electrician needs to build up the new set of wiring to co-exist alongside the old, until it is ready for the power to be switched over. If you are rewiring a whole house it is best to do it in stages so that, say, the downstairs is isolated and replaced before any work starts upstairs. You may periodically receive updates from the electrician as to which areas are working at any given time. His is a stressful job, because he is trying to minimise the disruption to anyone living and working in the property. However, with floorboards being taken up for joists to be drilled, and intermittent power cuts, there will always be overlaps between electricians ('sparkies') and other workers.

Plumbing

Most of the plumber's first fix is spent running pipework under floorboards or into walls and, rather like the electrician, constructing a parallel system to exist alongside the old one (often overcoming great difficulties in the process) until it is time to switch over the mains.

Central heating

Central heating engineers are different from general plumbers in that they have to be CORGI-registered (see Chapter 4). Any appliance which is connected by your builder or heating engineer to the gas supply inside the house has to be fitted by CORGI-registered personnel, who are assessed to carry out particular types of work: attaching the central heating boiler is usually the major job. For larger houses the boiler can be so large and heavy that it may require specialist lifting equipment, and perhaps the removal of a window frame to get it into the building. If you add a new boiler, you are also usually adding an entirely new system of pipes and radiators to every room as well. Gas-powered cookers, fires and warm-air heaters are also jobs for CORGI fitters.

Oil-fired systems

These require an enormously heavy boiler, plus an oil storage tank that holds from 200 to over 3,500 litres. These unsightly monsters are usually already in place, as they tend to outlast the boilers, but if you are putting one in then careful consideration needs to be given to where you can hide such a large object within easy reach of fuel-tanker access.

Electrical heating systems

Electricity, even on Economy 7 rates, currently leans towards the more expensive end of the heating spectrum. However, this could change as renewable sources such as wind farms and mass-produced photovoltaic panels become more widely available (the government target is that 10 per cent of energy should be generated from renewable sources by 2010). For more information see *The Which? Guide to the Energy-saving Home.*

Plastering

Towards the end of the first fix the plasterer arrives, which is both good news and bad news. Plastering represents significant progress and delivers one of the most noticeable steps forward towards the finished job; but it is also unbelievably messy. The spillage rate is phenomenal, and rooms which are being plastered, and even the routes into rooms being plastered, can be no-go areas for days. But plasterers make good the enormous mess left by the electricians and the plumbers, concealing the unsightly veins and arteries of the house beneath a smooth skim coat of recognisable, actual wall. On new walls they plaster up to (and sometimes over) light-switch and plug-socket boxes, and up to door and window frames; they will usually stop just short of the floor, where the gap will be covered by the skirting board. All these edges improve their appearance after the carpenter has been back and fitted the architraves and skirtings.

If you are having existing walls replastered whilst leaving the woodwork intact, for some reason no amount of sealed plastic sheeting will protect it. Somehow plaster permeates anything and you will probably be washing little lozenge-shaped splashes of plaster from all kinds of surfaces – balustrades, door handles, ceiling roses – for weeks afterwards. But it's worth it. When the plastering is finished the first fix is officially completed, which is a cause for celebration. This is the midpoint of the job, and the worst is behind. You might want to indulge in a celebratory takeaway.

The second fix

This is when the sun begins to shine again. All those things that you chose so carefully in what seems like a different, pre-building-works existence, such as bathroom fittings, radiators and sinks, start to go in, finally providing some positive evidence of your money being spent on something nice. The newly plastered walls provide a flattering backdrop for your excellent taste and suddenly the whole project starts to look more feasible. Doors are hung, kitchen units and light fittings go in, and finishing joinery work is carried out.

Recognisable rooms begin to emerge out of chaos, and all those door handles and taps you picked out, paid for and had forgotten about come out of their tissue paper like little jewels of progress, get set in place and represent parts of the job which are actually finished.

Watch out for accidental damage

There is still a way to go, and you must take care that vulnerable new fittings are not damaged by the continuing work around them. There is always someone rushing through at the last minute with a scaffold plank or a wheelbarrow, still in building-site mode, and just a tiny knock is enough to cause grievous damage to delicate home fittings. Often, masking tape is put around fixtures to prevent scratches. Better still is a rag, secured so that handles of cupboards and doors, etc. are still usable but given padded protection.

More plastering

With most of the plastering complete this is a very positive stage, involving fiddly areas that need to be finished off with a skim coat. This will again generate a lot of mess and may overlap with several other trades. Plumbers, electricians and decorators all wait on plasterers to finish, with ever more pressured allowances for drying time, before they can carry on with their work. Expect some grumbling from contractors.

Electrical fittings

At this point the electrician returns to put on fittings. Those light fittings you chose finally go on to the ceilings and walls (you have a wobbly moment, but no, they're fine). Crisp, clean light switches click on and off with the novelty of a new invention, and you know you're really getting there when you plug the kettle into a brand new socket outlet in the kitchen.

Plumbing

The plumber comes back to hang radiators on newly plastered walls, fit bathroom suites (or 'sanitaryware' as it is properly called) and the kitchen sink; check that things are level before he leaves. Suddenly you will feel that everything is starting to look fantastic.

Carpentry

The carpenter returns to fit architraves and skirting boards, hang doors, and finish any bespoke work he may be doing. If there is a kitchen involved, he is likely to be occupied with issues relating to worktops and units at this stage. Because of his absence during the intervening positive developments, the carpenter may seem somewhat diminished in your eyes, but he still has a very valuable contribution to make to the end result.

Flooring

Finishes such as parquet, or oak boards, are best laid as late as possible, since builders can add what seems like many years of wear to almost any surface.

Wall and floor tiling

Tilers are generally relatively sensitive types who, it has to be said, can sometimes be prima donnas. It is always unwise to generalise, but tilers do often seem to require absolutely perfect working conditions, or they will complain that they cannot function at all. Their work is skilled, and some would argue even has scope for artistic expression, but it is not rocket science. No single process is any more difficult than anything involved in wiring or plumbing, yet tilers' work is often presented as some sort of virtuoso performance for which the maestro must have absolute silence. It is also one of the trades that works the most closely, and falls out most often, with plumbers.

Decorators

Decorators are regarded as relatively unskilled within the building trade. Indeed many have other vocations. Temperamentally, decorators are different from the other trades: they are noticeably quieter to have around towards the end of the job, and tend to cause less shouting and (ironically for a potentially very messy finishing process) less mess.

Good decorators are able to become absorbed in their work in a way that a general builder who is offering his services as a decorator will not be able to match. Always ensure that if you are being charged for decorating work, it is skilled decoration that you are getting. Hands that tear down walls and build them up again seldom have the patience to produce a smooth, thoughtful professional finish.

Keep a snagging list

Make what is called a snagging list as you go around the site, noting any defects or deviations from your specification, or things you are not happy with, such as missing fittings, poor finishes, or gaps in the grouting.

A snagging list is an ongoing way of monitoring things which need to be rectified; you can also compile one at the end of a job. If you are employing a project manager, he will have one, but you can make your own too. If you have a project manager then you should show your list to him, not the builder, as this is the established procedure. If you are managing the project, raise matters tactfully. Builders understand about snagging lists and will not be offended or insulted to be told that there are things which need to be revisited, as long as this is handled correctly, ideally at a prearranged snagging meeting on site.

Chapter 8

Specific projects

Chapter 2 describes the Building Regulations and how to go about applying for planning permission, and advice on choosing a contractor is given in Chapter 4. In this section we examine special considerations to bear in mind when undertaking some of the most popular building projects, including compliance with the law, common problems and what to expect while work is in progress.

Kitchen refitting

The kitchen is used for up to 80 per cent of the day, morning, noon and night. It is the hub of the house, and often the best room at parties. Whether you are putting in a new kitchen or adapting an old one, it should be designed to be as spacious as possible, with easy circulation between the three essential facilities of fridge, sink and cooker; and also to look good and increase the value of the house. Wonky worktops, cupboard doors which do not close properly and bad ergonomics all make people lose faith in a kitchen and cast doubt on its capacity to produce culinary alchemy. When general builders venture into the relatively delicate area of kitchen design and installation, the results can seem heavy-handed.

Sometimes only a partial refit is necessary. This makes do with much of the existing underlying kitchen. Underneath the worktops and behind the cupboard doors you will usually find white, or brown, melamine box units, called carcasses, screwed to the wall. If these are not necessarily worn out or in the wrong place, you may not need to take them out. New worktops and doors, along with a rethink of appliances, can make a world of difference. However, a total refit allows you to sort out problems which may have been bothering you for years. Now is your chance finally to have a socket for the kettle, the toaster and the microwave, without them all having to share one double socket.

What shape should the kitchen be?

There are several traditional options for kitchen layouts, including the following.

- **The single-line layout** groups everything in the room along one straight wall – this is not generally a practical solution, except in very small rooms with minimal facilities.
- **The galley kitchen** usually has sink, cooker and some worktops along one wall, and food storage and preparation areas along the opposite wall. This layout can work well, but if the room is a through route to the back door, you will need plenty of floor space down the middle of it.
- **The L-shaped room** has fixtures and fittings along two adjacent walls. This can be very effective, providing space in the opposite corner of the room for a table and chairs if the room is big enough, as well as separating the work areas from any through traffic to the back door.
- **The U-shaped room** has its equipment and worktops ranged along three walls. It is a highly efficient plan, and can be used to link kitchen and dining areas if one section of the 'U' acts as a peninsula unit. However, this layout can entail a lot of walking about if the room is large, and, in a small room, can be very cramped for more people than just one cook and bottle-washer.
- **The island layout** sites units or a table in the centre of an L- or U-shaped floor plan. This can be very effective in a kitchen which is used a great deal for family activities, but needs careful planning and plenty of space in order to avoid a troublesome congestion of people round the island.

Building Regulations

Building Regulations approval is not needed when altering a kitchen if all you are doing is replacing the old equipment and fittings with new ones. If you are making any alterations to the existing waste-water disposal arrangements, however, or are fitting a heating appliance where none existed before, you will need approval for the new work. Additional ventilation may also be required, which may necessitate a visit from a CORGI* -approved engineer to test that the new airflow has not altered the potential for carbon monoxide emissions from your cooker, combi boiler or other appliances.

Socket outlets must be sited at least one metre from the sink in order to reduce the risk of dropping the kettle into the washing-up while it is still plugged in.

Planning permission

This is not usually necessary unless you are extending the building.

The most common problems

- **Plumbing restrictions** Even if you are starting from scratch there will still be basic limitations – on the siting of the sink, for instance. Ideally sinks should go against an outside wall for drainage, and not be tucked into a corner where they can be difficult to reach.
- **Trying to squeeze in too many appliances** This causes a lot of problems as each one reduces available cupboard space and monopolises an area of floor space when in use. Also, the wide, open spaces of the worktops in your drawings will soon become crowded by that microwave, toaster and kettle (even if they do have their own sockets). Then there's that juicer you never use, the radio, and the ubiquitous food mixer, which does have its place in the kitchen but could probably be stored in a cupboard.
- **Laundry** Do you really need to do the laundry in the kitchen? Check if there is a possibility of moving this space-consuming process into another room. A scullery, pantry, conservatory, or a large underused upstairs airing cupboard perhaps.

The biggest problem: disruption

Doing without a kitchen for the duration of the changeover can be extremely disruptive. It is astonishing how much time we spend in the kitchen and how often we visit it every day. It's hard to imagine the inconvenience of not being able to pop to the fridge, rinse your hands under the tap, or just stare out of the kitchen window nursing a cup of tea. For these home comforts it may be best to take refuge with a neighbour, because even if you can keep the fridge operational in the hall, cooking anything properly is out of the question. Some people retreat to a hotel for the duration, but you should at least treat yourself to a takeaway every day you are without facilities.

A contractor who is familiar with re-fitting kitchens will consider this and make sure you are not left without the basic facilities whenever possible.

The sequence of events

1. **Stripping out** Kitchen units are usually straightforward to remove, and you shouldn't need to take a crowbar to them. Most are held in place with two screws, and time spent carefully unscrewing these can mean time saved in replastering the wall. Once walls have been re-plastered where necessary, walls and ceilings should be painted.
2. **The electrics are installed** New appliances such as fridge-freezers, dishwashers, washer-driers and waste-disposal units all create new demands on the wiring, which is generally best upgraded to a 30-amp ring circuit. Electric ovens and cookers will need a 45-amp circuit all of their own.
3. **Installing new cables and socket outlets** This can involve fairly considerable masonry excavation. Most plumbing should run along the back of the units, out of sight, against an outside wall. Its position will often dictate the final layout of appliances such as dishwashers and washing machines.
4. **New unit assembly** This should not be a problem unless you are having to modify the units – which are almost always 600mm deep and 300mm to 1,000mm wide – or having bespoke units made.
5. **Worktops and finishes are put in place** Granite, stainless steel, wood or composite worktops can be made to measure off site and sometimes installed in an afternoon.
6. **Worktops are sealed** Taps are fitted and tiling put in place.

Timescale: between two and three weeks.

The case for using a specialist

A kitchen specialist will appreciate that it is unreasonable to deprive the family living in the house of kitchen facilities for any longer than necessary. They generally manage to create another temporary kitchen, made up out of the component parts of the old kitchen, dismantled and reassembled in a temporary area, with washing and cooking facilities if possible, to minimise disruption during the changeover from old to new facilities. A good firm will aim to keep this actual changeover period as short as possible – for instance a day, perhaps even half a day.

The main skill needed in kitchen fitting is carpentry – coping with the fact that house walls are neither flat, straight or square to one another, and fitting units and worktops into spaces that are not quite the right size. Whether or not you need a specialist plumber and electrician depends on how much extra work is involved – most kitchen fitters will be able to do the basics.

Finding a specialist kitchen fitter

One way to guarantee you get someone who has done it before is to buy your kitchen from one of the big kitchen showrooms. Their fitters will be among the most proficient in the business, and may well have fitted exactly the same kitchen into a similar property only the week before. Alternatively, a lot of people prefer to go for something more individual. It is still possible to find a professional fitter through the routes outlined in Chapter 4, by searching the directories, or asking in smaller or medium-sized kitchen showrooms if they can recommend fitters who do private domestic work.

Bathrooms

Improving bathroom facilities is one of the most popular home improvement projects. In its simplest form, the job involves replacing like with like: taking out the old appliances and installing new ones in their place. The benefits are largely aesthetic – you can choose the equipment in a colour and style that you like – but there are also practical gains in having new, easy-to-clean surfaces, and taps that do not drip or seize up. The job is not difficult, but can be time-consuming when it comes to marrying up new equipment to old supply and waste pipes.

The project becomes more complex if you want to change the layout of the room, or to take a radical decision such as doing away with the bath in favour of a shower cubicle and more free floor space. In such instances, some careful planning of the way in which you use the bathroom floor space is called for. The creation of extra space may be possible if you are able to reposition the bathroom door.

Much the same as with the kitchen, you can't afford to be without a bathroom for very long. Critical to your quality of life will be the speed and efficiency of the changeover from old to new basic facilities, as well as the smoothness of the implementation of your final design.

Bathroom planning

Whether you are planning to change the layout of an existing bathroom, or are creating new facilities, you must be aware of the need to retain free floor space in order to allow the various appliances to be used in comfort; this is known as 'activity space'. You need room beside a bath, for example, so you can step in and out of it, stand next to it to dry yourself, and perhaps kneel beside it to bathe a child. Similarly, you need elbow room when standing at a washbasin so that you can wash your hair and clean your teeth without your elbows hitting a side wall.

Note that activity spaces between adjacent appliances may overlap slightly in practice, especially where they are unlikely to be in use at the same time. The full width of the activity space in front of a washbasin is needed only at waist level and above so if necessary it could intrude over an adjacent bath or WC, for example.

The best way of planning a bathroom layout is to make scale drawings on squared paper. Draw individual pieces of equipment to scale, adding an area indicating the necessary activity space for each, cut them out, and then move them round a scale plan of the room until you reach the best practical arrangement. You can get help with bathroom planning from many bathroom showrooms.

Building Regulations

Building Regulations approval is not needed if you are simply replacing the old equipment and fittings with new ones. If you are altering the existing waste-water disposal arrangements, however, or are fitting a new heating appliance, you will need approval for the new work.

You will also need approval if you are partitioning a WC from an existing bathroom, installing a second WC, or fitting washbasins or shower cubicles into bedrooms, because new waste pipes will have to be installed. In the case of new WC cubicles, the Regulations ventilation requirements must also be met.

The Regulations allow the use of a pumped macerator unit and small-bore pipework if the siting of the new appliances makes running conventional soil and waste pipes difficult. Don't forget that bidets and appliances such as jacuzzi baths create the potential for back siphonage to occur (where dirty water is sucked into the mains in times of high demand) and so the water company must be notified before they are installed.

The most common problems

- **Spillages in the changeover** A good plumber keeps a supply of rags handy at all times and deploys a drip tray.
- **New taps and fittings** Sometimes these don't quite fit the new sanitaryware (bath, basin and bidet) and need to be rethought. British taps and sanitaryware should be made to the same standards but the Italian and French ones which are offered in showrooms in the UK are sometimes not compatible with appliances sold by the same showroom, which they won't necessarily tell you because they might not know themselves.
- **Coordinating the tiler and plumber** These two trades are temperamentally diametrically opposed, and always in demand elsewhere.

The biggest problem: drainage pipes

Getting the drainage flow right, particularly if you are altering the layout of the room, can be tricky. Pipes which are too steeply inclined can make an unpleasant noise and will empty traps of water, and those at too shallow a gradient can take an age to drain, smell of stagnant water and be prone to blockages. There can also be problems fitting traps – especially under shower trays – where space is limited.

The sequence of events

1. **New pipework is made up** and laid ready to be joined to the existing system.
2. **Water is drained from the toilet** and this is removed, along with the hand basin, bath and, if you have one, the bidet.
3. **Painting, wallpapering and fitting of bathroom furniture** (cupboards) should all be done next.
4. **Taps are fitted** to the new bath, basin and bidet, which are placed in position before being secured in place.
5. **The all-important waste pipes are connected** first, then the water supply, which ensures that that first experimental run of the tap doesn't pass through an open plughole and end up on your feet.
6. **Tiling** is completed.

Timescale: two to eight weeks depending on the size of the job and the number of unforeseen circumstances you encounter.

The case for using a specialist

Any general builder should be able to put in a bathroom blindfolded, but sometimes when you see the finished article you wonder if maybe he was. Changing over a toilet should be straightforward, but it's not unknown for people to have to employ a specialist to replace a cracked cast-iron soil stack because a general builder has hit it with his hammer.

Getting basins and baths level so that they drain correctly, and look right – and getting things squared to the wall properly, even when the wall isn't actually square – are the main differences when you employ a specialist. With a bit of experience, and mastic, a specialist can make even the oddest-shaped room look right. General builders might use grout for sealing around a bath or shower tray rather than flexible silicone sealant (which is more difficult to use). It looks great for a bit, but will crack when the bath or shower tray inevitably moves. The other advantages of using specialists are speed, and costs in time and materials.

Finding a specialist bathroom fitter

Specialist bathroom fitters often advertise in *Yellow Pages*. As well as relying on recommendation you should check for membership of organisations such as The Kitchen Bathroom Bedroom Specialists Association (KBSA)*.

Bathroom blunders

One 'rookie' mistake is to finish all the tiling before the thermostatic mixer valve on a concealed shower unit has been properly tested. The shower will run hot and cold, which is tested for, but it won't mix. So when the customer has his inaugural shower he will not be amused to be alternately scalded and frozen. These valves are delicate and easily damaged if installed incorrectly, so it may be necessary to go back into the tiled wall to refit it at the builder's expense – and the customer's inconvenience.

Loft conversions

Although an empty loft can seem like an open invitation to extend your living area, loft conversions can be quite tricky. They usually involve dealing with an older, established structure and reorganising the loads it has to cope with. The change of usage in the top part of the building may have unanticipated knock-on effects elsewhere if not properly thought out. Perhaps most importantly, you are interfering with the main waterproofing of the house. If this goes wrong, it can have serious, long-term implications for the fabric of the building.

Unless the building firm hires scaffolding or a crane, access for building materials to the work site is restricted to what can be carried through the house, and use of the space itself may be hampered by a number of factors. For example, as it is often prohibited for dormer windows to face the road, because this counts as a development 'overlooking the public highway', it is a common aspiration to insert bathroom facilities under the front eaves, and put the main rooms in the roomier, rear-facing dormer area. But drainage pipes and soil stacks are usually positioned at the side or the back of the house, and running a soil stack from one side of the house to the other is often impractical (especially at right angles to the joists) and not allowed. The Building Regulations allow the use of a pumped macerator unit and small-bore pipework if the siting of appliances makes running conventional soil and waste pipes difficult. Shredding and pumping units, such as Saniflo, originally designed for boats, don't need a large-bore soil pipe and work more or less anywhere.

Assessing the feasibility of conversion

Whether you can actually convert your loft depends on the structure of the roof of your house. Until the 1960s, pitched roofs were constructed on site from a framework of rafters (the sloping beams that support the roof's covering), purlins (the horizontal beams that tie the rafters together) and struts (which brace the purlins against the first-floor ceiling joists and any internal load-bearing walls). Viewed from within the loft, such a roof structure may look like an awkward place in which to fit a new room, but it can generally be easily adapted by relocating the struts and other components within the roof's space. However, this is a job that needs professional assessment in order to ensure that the alterations do not weaken the roof's structure.

In more recently built houses, the roof is usually constructed with roof trusses. These are prefabricated, triangular, timber frames that span the walls of the main house, thereby removing the need for internal load-bearing walls. The way in which the trusses are erected and braced, however, means that removing any of their components will seriously weaken the roof's structure, and therefore altering it to allow the creation of loft rooms will be difficult and expensive. Unless you are prepared to go to these lengths, all that you can realistically do is to provide improved access to, and lighting of, the roof space, and then use it for storage purposes.

Building Regulations

Loft conversions always need Building Regulations approval in order to make sure that the alterations satisfy the requirements concerning structural stability, safe access, thermal insulation, ventilation, fireproofing, waste disposal (if the conversion will contain sanitary facilities), and, above all, means of escape in the event of fire.

Fire regulations involving sprung door-closing devices, door-width specifications and the 'no room off a room' rule may appear to exist to thwart the feng shui of your plans, but save lives.

You must deposit full plans, not just a building notice, if you are converting a two-storey building.

Planning permission

This is mandatory in Scotland, but not normally necessary for a loft conversion in England and Wales unless:

- dormer windows or other alterations to the shape of the roof will face a highway
- the height of the roof will increase
- the volume of the building will be increased by more than 50 cu m, or 40 cu m for a terraced house. Note that this volume counts against your overall permitted development rights (see page 32).

Permission may be required if the building is listed or in a Conservation Area (see Chapter 2).

Building Regulations

In most houses the loft space was not originally designed for occupancy, and the change of function involves far more work, and consequently regulation, than most people imagine. Structural stability, access, insulation, ventilation and drainage (if applicable) are all tightly controlled, but the most important – and potentially most restrictive – regulations are for fire.

The fire rating, which is the amount of time for which a material can resist the spread of fire, is specified on many materials used in converting a loft, such as doors, glass and insulation, and can also relate to the actual construction of partitions and floors. In a loft conversion it is often necessary to upgrade the fire resistance of existing floors and doors leading off the stairway. Having a 'means of escape' is vitally important. If there is no space in the downstairs hall to accommodate the staircase, this can sometimes completely scupper a loft-conversion plan. It is not possible to site a staircase within a room off the hall because this counts as a 'room off a room', which doesn't provide a proper means of escape. If you have to move a wall to accommodate the staircase, you will be entering a whole new world of regulation.

Letting in light

The two most common ways of creating windows in loft rooms are to install some in the plane of the roof's slope, or to build projecting dormers. Roof windows are designed in sizes that match the standard rafter spacings; narrow models fit between adjacent pairs of rafters, while wider ones require the removal of a section of rafter. Dormer windows are built out from the roof's slope, and have a conventional, vertical window fitted between the sides of the dormer under a flat, sloping or ridged dormer roof. So-called 'bay' dormers extend to the eaves, and help to create additional headroom within the loft. In theory, a dormer can also span the full width of the property, but this rarely looks attractive, and you may have trouble getting your local planning authority to agree to the scheme.

The most common problems

- **Keeping the floor level down to maximise the ceiling height** It is very rare to get permission to develop above the established roof line, and most houses in the UK have a fairly low roof ridge. Very careful consideration needs to be given to the thickness of the beams and joists strengthening the floor, because every inch could be critical. Loft specialists routinely use wider beams, which are less deep than conventional supports.
- **Positioning the staircase** This affects how the room is used upstairs, and the floor space of the floor below. Be cautious if a general builder advises you to take out a wall specifically to site the staircase. This may not be necessary, and is probably not advisable if you are not planning to change the use of the downstairs rooms. There are several types of staircase available for use in loft conversions – including spiral staircases, box staircases and 'space saver' stairs (with alternate paddle-shaped treads) – all of which take up less room than a conventional staircase and should be considered if you have a problem. Specialist loft conversion

suppliers (see below) have a good selection of these. A loft conversion must have a permanent staircase, not a loft ladder.

- **Strength of walls** Are the walls strong enough to cope with the increased pressure caused by the extra load? Roof spread, where the weight of the roof presses the walls outwards, can be an issue if the purlins, the cross supports within the roof, are adapted to create more space. This creates new 'vertical load paths' which the walls need to be able to bear. If they cannot, then reinforcing them with ties can be costly and unsightly, and can reduce a prospective buyer's confidence in the building.

The biggest problem: Building Regulations compliance

- **Planning** There are tight Building Regulations governing means of escape in case of fire (see page 115). Often this may mean upgrading the fire protection of existing floors, doors and walls rather than putting in an actual fire escape.
- **Neighbours** People living nearby, or perhaps even in the same building where the work is taking place, may have the inclination – and the right – to object to something which will inevitably inconvenience them. Most people are generally magnanimous, but there are people who can be difficult. People with a share of the freehold, for instance, may have a right of veto over the development of a loft, even if they live in separate flats, have no right of access and would not be affected by its development in any way.

The sequence of events

1. **Creating the access** This can initially mean a secured ladder during the works, but when it is time to install the staircase, loft converters recommend using a specialist firm for its manufacture and positioning. Making successful use of the space depends on where the staircase is sited.
2. **Strengthening the structure** Once access is in place, the beams or rolled steel joists (RSJs) which will strengthen the structure can be carried up. Although the ceiling joists inside the loft may look strong, they are usually designed to carry only the weight of the ceiling below, and will almost certainly require reinforcement if the extra weight of a new room is imposed. Roof support timbers are also repositioned at this stage.

3. **Access is made for windows** (dormer or roof window or both). The hole in the roof can seem a bit alarming in its raw state, but the transformation of the room brought about by the new rush of light more than makes up for it. Peering out of a gap in your own roof is heady stuff. When choosing your window, don't forget to plan how you are going to clean it.

4. **Insulation** Money spent on the careful siting of good-quality products here will soon come back to you in lower heating bills. You may, in fact, have little choice over what you fit, as Building Regulations cover insulation in lofts in some detail.

5. **The internal walls go in**, if applicable – although the joy of a loft is often that there aren't any internal walls and the light, airy space benefits from the whole of the building's footprint as its floor area.

6. **Wiring and plumbing services** can usually be extended from the existing supply, though the header and storage tanks will almost certainly need to be resited to the eaves.

7. **Plastering**, decorating, inhabiting.

Timescale: four to six months, from planning to completion.

The case for using a specialist

When you poke your head into your loft for the first time with an eye to conversion, it is easy to see it as a finished room. There is a floor, a roof, and usually a lot of unused space with the potential for developing a lot more. However, things are seldom as simple as they seem, and a general builder may soon get bogged down in the extensive Building Regulation requirements, and the logistical difficulties of working at the top of a house that people are living in. In addition you want the finished product to be sympathetic to the rest of the building, or it may end up looking like a shoddy add-on rather than the value-enhancing feature you intended. For these reasons, no matter how simple the job seems, a specialist is always infinitely preferable to a general builder.

In London, for instance, different boroughs can have diametrically opposed policies on issues such as whether dormers can face the road, and whether you are allowed to run them gable end to gable end or just have isolated windows. Boroughs which border each other may have completely opposite policies, so that one side of the road looks totally different from the other. One tried-and-tested means of blocking dormer window applications, and thus pouring cold water on the whole conversion, is to check old Ordnance Survey maps to see whether there might be a path, even an ancient one, long forgotten and overgrown, running along the bottom of your garden – which counts as overlooking the public highway. A specialist will be able to advise on the local restrictions and regulations and work around the planners to ensure that as far as possible you get the desired result.

If the work involves a party wall, which it very often does, you need to notify the other people involved (see page 82). A general builder might leave this to the Royal Institution of Chartered Surveyors (RICS)★. However, the party-wall notification document that the organisation sends out looks like a summons and requests a response within a certain time. It could alarm the recipient, and may spark a dispute. A big disagreement means employing party-wall surveyors on both sides, plus a third, independent expert observer, which can cause considerable expense. Specialists know that a personal letter letting your neighbours know your intentions can achieve results more effectively.

Finding a loft conversion specialist

You could ask the Federation of Master Builders (FMB)★ or another registration scheme for a list of members who specialise in loft conversions – see Appendix I. Trussloft Ltd★ claims to be the UK's only national loft conversion company.

Alternatively the Loft Shop★ is a chain in the south-east of England which stocks everything you need to convert your loft off the shelf, and will provide a quote on bespoke items. Loft Centre Products★ will supply to anywhere in the country.

An inside insight

One specialist reckons it is surprising how little some planners know about loft conversions. 'I took a group of planners from one London borough around some conversions that I'd done to show them the sort of thing that is achievable, and they were saying things such as: "Oh, is this a conversion, then?" It turned out that the man who set one council's entire policy on loft conversions had never actually been in one.'

Basements and cellars

Many older houses have either a basement or a cellar. Basements were generally intended for use as kitchens and sculleries, or for similar purposes, by live-in staff. Cellars, on the other hand, were generally built under only part of the house, and their access was always just from inside the house (perhaps with a coal hole for deliveries). A typical cellar has no natural light or ventilation, and may possess only the most rudimentary damp-proofing. A basement clearly offers more scope for conversion into habitable rooms.

Structural work needs Building Regulations approval (you can use the building notice scheme instead of applying for written approval if you are confident your plans meet the Regulations). You also need approval if you are installing new sanitary or fuel-burning appliances, and any wiring work carried out should meet Wiring Regulations. A conversion will not need planning permission unless a change of use is involved: to a home office, a self-contained flat or a garage, for example.

The major problem is likely to be that of damp (have a professional survey done). Work will involve putting down a polythene damp-proof membrane and perhaps a new floor, damp-proofing the walls, perhaps fitting a new staircase, and installing or upgrading services. It is generally best to fit independent heaters. Balanced-flue gas heaters are ideal in a basement conversion in which the flues can discharge their emissions into the outside air; electricity is best in a cellar conversion.

Conservatories

A conservatory is defined as having a transparent or translucent roof. It is a relatively painless structural addition in that as most of the work takes place outside the house, conservatories are mostly exempt from Building Regulations (see below), and the duration of the job is relatively short. Building a conservatory is much cheaper than a brick-and-block or timber frame extension and when complete it often turns out to be an extremely versatile room which, if properly designed, can increase the value and appeal of a property. If the proper materials are used, and suffi-cient attention is paid to the heating and ventilation, then a con-servatory can soon become one of the most lived-in rooms in the house.

Building Regulations

In England, Wales and Northern Ireland but not Scotland, the structures of smaller conservatories are exempt from Building Regulations control provided their floor area does not exceed 30sq m (325sq ft). Other rules may apply:

- safety glass must be used in doors and low-level glazing in the conservatory to comply with Part N of the Regulations
- structural alterations creating new access routes into the con-servatory from the house must comply with parts A and L
- there must be ventilation openings (such as patio doors or French windows) in the conservatory, and in any habitable room that will be ventilated through it, to comply with Part F of the Regulations. The doors must have an opening area equal to five per cent of the combined floor area of the two rooms. In addition, each room must have background ventilation, with a minimum open area of 8,000sq mm (12sq in)

Planning permission

Some people may tell you that a conservatory does not require plan-ning permission because it is classed as a 'temporary structure', but if you listen to them then you should also listen out for the sound of breaking glass as the council's JCB razes your illegal conservatory to the ground. A conservatory counts as an extension to a building, so planning permission will be necessary if:

- your proposed extension or conservatory increases the volume of the house by more than your permitted development rights – see Chapter 2
- your permitted development rights were surrendered in order to obtain the original planning permission for the building
- the extension or conservatory is closer than 2 m to the boundary with your neighbours and more than 4 m high
- it is higher than any part of the original structure

- it projects from the front of the house towards the highway, or towards a footpath at the back (this may mean one that is long-forgotten), unless there would be at least 20 m between it and the highway or footpath
- it will take up more than half of the garden
- your deeds forbid it. Sometimes deeds have restrictive covenants inserted to preclude any further development, particularly in multi-occupancy dwellings where the freehold is shared or operated by a limited company. Take legal advice as to whether it is possible to have these covenants put aside.

The most common problems

- **Water penetration** See below.
- **Ventilation** A certain degree of ventilation is specified in the Building Regulations, but if you want to be sure you don't wilt in the summer months (bearing in mind that the UK climate is getting hotter), you might want to consider fans, blinds and roof panels that open – as well as openable windows.
- **Heating** In the winter even double glazing saps heat fast, so some kind of heating is necessary to prevent the conservatory from becoming a no-go area due to the cold. Under-floor heating is one option; extending the existing central heating (with one or more radiators or heaters in the conservatory) is another.
- **Cleaning and maintenance** How are you going to clean the conservatory, particularly the roof? Are the sides strong enough to support a ladder leaning up against them? Will the roof take your weight if it is spread across a board or plank? Is this a safe option? Most conservatory owners end up investing in a mop with a very long handle. Your installer will be able to advise you on cleaning methods.
- **Access to other windows** How are you going to clean or paint any first-floor or second-storey windows above the conservatory? One solution to this is to replace any windows above the conservatory with maintenance-free windows (painted aluminium or PVC-U, for example). Reversible hinges allow both sides of the window to be cleaned from the inside. Otherwise, scaffolding over the conservatory may be needed. Note that conservatories should not be placed so that ladders cannot be

put up to high windows (in a loft conversion, for example) that are intended as means of escape in the event of fire.

- **Security** How good are the locks? Will the structure compromise security? Ideally, secure locks should be fitted to a conservatory from the start. It is possible to add extra locks if the original ones are inadequate. This may be a good time to install motion detector-activated security lighting. This could make you unpopular with your neighbours, however, as every passing cat, fox and badger may activate it.

- **Manholes** If your conservatory covers one of these, you will have to get digging to make another one – and limber up your wrist for some serious form filling as manholes (inspection chambers) are covered by the Building Regulations. Alternatively you could have a double-seal cover on the existing manhole.

- **Downpipes and soil pipes within the site** Generally conservatories are located on areas of the building which are free from downpipes and soil pipes, but if there is no other option these pipes can be moved. This can be a time-consuming, ugly (and smelly) business which may require permission, and should not be embarked upon lightly.

The biggest problem: water penetration

One of the most common reasons for a surveyor to be called upon to provide expert testimony is water penetration in conservatories. Because conservatories are lightweight constructions without structural regulations, general builders often assume that a strip of lead (flashing) set half an inch into the mortar will be sufficient to seal the join. However, water can penetrate the external wall higher up, above the flashing, and run down on the inside of the cavity wall. This moisture will then re-emerge through what used to be the external wall, but is now the finely skim-plastered and wallpapered back wall of your new conservatory. Bubbles in the plaster (and flickering wall lights) mean that moisture has penetrated. The only answer is chiselling out a row of bricks above the flashing and installing a cavity tray, which must catch the rain and channel it away from the conservatory. Ideally this should be done before the conservatory roof glazing goes in, rather than afterwards.

123

The sequence of events

1. **The site is cleared and excavated** This means levelling off the ground, repositioning downpipes, etc.
2. **Foundations are laid** and a 'dwarf' wall, to carry the walls of the conservatory, built incorporating a damp-proof course (DPC). The existing outside wall (soon to become the inside wall) should already have a DPC installed.
3. **The base is put down** There are no Building Regulations to be met, but the specific instructions from the conservatory manufacturer should be followed carefully. A concrete base 75–150mm below the DPC is advisable. Channels should be left in the base for ducts leading to airbricks (if the conservatory base would otherwise cover these up) and for electric wiring and central heating pipes if required.
4. **The structure is erected** This is usually modular steel, aluminium, PVC or timber. Weatherproofing the join is usually done using lead flashing, which should be tucked a full inch into the mortar.
5. **The cavity tray is installed**, if you are having one (see above).
6. **Roof and side panels are glazed**.
7. **The electrical supply** is connected, wall lights are fitted and wired up, the ceiling fan connected and the electrical supply connected to the mains. The heating radiators are connected up.
8. **Plastering (if required), finishes (painting, varnishing woodwork and floor treatments) and flooring** Plastering will conceal any electrical cables or plumbing work, though many people leave the existing wall finish as bare brick, render, stucco or pebbledash.

Timescale: Approximately six weeks.

The case for using a specialist

You may buy a conservatory, and then find a contractor – perhaps the conservatory manufacturer can recommend one. Or you may rely on a specialist firm to provide and build the structure.

If you use a general builder to fit a conservatory, it will probably end up being more expensive than employing a specialist. For a start, he might have to pay more for the materials: a specialist will deal with a conservatory supplier maybe 20 or 30 times a year, and is likely to get a better deal than a contractor making a one-off pur-chase. Also, the general builder will be at a disadvantage regarding the speed of his deliveries, and will probably accomplish the job more slowly. Full-time fitters know what they are doing when it comes to glazing and will routinely use superior grades of glass, with better thermal and energy-saving properties.

Finding a conservatory specialist

The Conservatory Association* is a trade body with a national data-base of 300 members who can supply and install conservatories. They have a code of practice and occasionally expel members for deviating from it, though most of their calls are for advice from consumers who have employed non-members.

Building a home extension

An extension can often seem like the perfect solution for a cramped house, but one very important thing to consider when planning an extension is exactly what you are going to use the extra space for. If you need an extra bedroom then its function will be clear, but, sur-prisingly, misunderstandings about an extension's purpose between couples, and within families, can remain until well into the con-struction stage. Is it going to be a play room? A study? Or a larger lounge? Or has someone else in the household got their eye on it for some entirely different function, like table-tennis or sewing? It is best to get these things ironed out before you move in the furni-ture, or you could find yourself playing ping-pong while someone tries to make a dress down at the other end of the table.

One unexpected advantage of extensions is that they can some-times dramatically free up other areas of the house. Something like a large kitchen extension, for instance, with a portable television in it, can suddenly act as a magnet for younger, noisier and perhaps more fridge-oriented members of the household, who then free up the formerly overcrowded lounge for their parents – perhaps a final armistice in the battle for the remote.

Building Regulations

Extensions almost always require Building Regulations approval, particularly brick-built ones with habitable rooms like the one that most people plan: so prepare to have your wilder ideas curtailed. You will have to apply for approval from your local authority (see page 31 for full details of exactly what is involved).

Planning permission

This is usually required if you have used up your permitted development allowance – the volume by which you are permitted to increase the original house (see page 32).

As long as it falls within the permitted allowance, the extension will not need planning permission if it complies with the following additional conditions:

- it must not project above the original roof line of the house, nor in front of any house wall facing a highway
- it must not exceed 4m (13ft) in overall height if it will be built within 2 m (6ft, 6 in) of a boundary
- it must not result in more than half the site being built on.

If the allowance has been used, permission may still be granted if a good case can be made that your proposals fit within the planning guidelines. Local architects who are familiar with the local requirements – and the tastes of individual planning officers – may be able to assist in getting a sympathetic addition approved, particularly if a precedent has been set nearby. For more on appointing an architect, see Chapter 3.

Note that if the extension is built to provide facilities such as a self-contained granny flat or a home office, planning permission may be needed to cover the change of use, even if the extension itself comes within the permitted development rules. Check this out at an early stage.

Remember, too, that there may be circumstances in which your permitted development rights have been removed: for example, as a condition of a previous planning consent, such as that granted when the house was first built.

The most common problems

- **Matching the extension to the original design of the house** In some areas, it may be compulsory to use local stone. A problem with houses built with imperial 9 in bricks used up to around the mid-1970s is that bricks are now standardised at 225mm, which is ever so slightly smaller. It's the small (1.7mm) difference in height that is the main problem. This soon adds up, so that the add-on is always noticeable, particularly to obsessive brick-watchers, of whom there are surprisingly many – as extension owners tend to discover. You have three choices: make the mortar course thicker so that the brick courses line up; ignore the problem; or use second-hand (reclaimed) bricks, which may also have the advantage that they are already weathered and match the existing bricks. There is a huge choice of bricks available – you can find brick 'libraries' on the Internet – and you should be able to get something suitable. Well-chosen bricks 'weather in' and become indistinguishable from the main house over a period of several years. Alternatively you could deliberately choose to have your extension in a contrasting colour – though this approach may not be possible if you live in a listed building or Conservation Area (see page 32), in which case you may only be allowed to use certain brick bonding patterns and types of lintels and plinths.

- **Siting the extension** You need to find a good place on the outside of the building that will match your internal requirements and which fits with the requirements for planning permission. If your house is of a fairly common type in the area, it will be well worth touring your neighbourhood to look at other extensions. If one really catches your eye, then the person who commissioned it will almost certainly be pleased to talk to you about it and perhaps hand you the details of both the architect and the builders who built it.

- **Getting the roof right** If you are adding to the gable end of a house, try to follow the slope of the existing roof and match the tiles or slates. A pitched roof with good-quality slates, for instance, often accounts for a significant proportion of the cost of the extension. But if your existing house adopts this style, then something like a flat felt roof would be a false economy, drawing attention to the add-on and making it look like a prefabricated hut. You may be able to pitch the new roof at right angles to the existing one – and get away with using man-made slates, some of which are very realistic. Man-made slates are much lighter than traditional ones and are significantly less expensive.

- **Windows** It is important to try to match the style and height of the windows used in the extension to those used on the adjacent elevation of the house. Keeping the windows' head and sill levels the same will go a long way towards unifying the appearance of the old and new buildings. This applies particularly to older houses, in which modern casement windows would look completely incongruous next to original sash windows. If you cannot find an off-the-shelf match, consider having your new windows made to measure.

The biggest problem: good design

Apart from the problem of getting planning permission, which can range from being straightforward to very awkward indeed, extensions can suffer from access problems between the old and the new sections of the house, and create traffic-flow problems elsewhere if they are poorly designed. The new room might become extremely popular and create demands on passageways or thoroughfares which were not there before, but which now need to be accommodated. You can also make an existing room significantly darker if an existing window is used to create a doorway into the extension. Your design will be controlled in terms of access routes, fire risk, lighting, power and ventilation but no one in Building Control will stop you from proceeding with something which may turn out to be impractical. An architect will be skilled at anticipating potential problems. For more on employing one, see page 47.

The sequence of events

1. **The site is cleared** This could range from demolishing an existing structure to simply tidying up the lawn. Decisions about storing materials and tools have to be made and the area of the foundations marked out.
2. **Digging commences** Extensions generally require deep foundations and extra drainage, including that for the extra water coming off the roof – all of which generally means that a lot of mud has to be dug up and transported out of the garden.
3. **The walls go up** Block or brick walls are labour-intensive to construct, but this can be one of the most dramatic and

rewarding stages of any job to witness. In a timber-frame construction, the inner walls appear as if by magic.

4. **Upper-floor joists** are built in.
5. **The roof is added** Waterproofing the structure is a time-consuming but highly significant stage, at the end of which it all starts to look like a real house again – only bigger.
6. **Wiring, plumbing and heating** are put in place. Supplying these services is usually straightforward. You should be able to run new socket outlets off the existing ring circuit, provided the total area served by the whole ring is not more than 100sq m, but a new kitchen extension should have its own new socket outlet circuit. Existing lighting circuits can usually be extended too, and most boilers have the capacity to support extra radiators.
7. **Plastering** is carried out – the last of the really messy processes.
8. **Skirtings and decorating** are completed. These are tasks which many people like to tackle themselves, to save money and to take possession of the project at the earliest possible moment.

Timescale: Usually eight to twelve months from planning to completion. It can be a longer process.

The case for using a specialist

Employing an architect and/or builder who specialises in extensions and who knows the ropes in a given area can offer significant benefits. People in sensitive planning areas can be over-cautious and apply for a construction hardly bigger than a porch. A specialist will know exactly what is permissible, who to approach, and how to keep the Building Control Officer happy. A specialist will also be more skilled in that vital art – making the extension look as though it is part of the original house.

The relationship with your contractor can be smoother if you employ someone who has been through all the stages of the job with a large number of customers. Large-scale building work in the home is quite an upheaval: a specialist will be able to anticipate at which stages the customer is likely to get stressed and upset, and is more likely to handle matters sensitively. If the builder is encountering problems and getting flustered himself, he may pass that on to the client, which makes for a less pleasant job.

Finding an extension specialist

The Federation of Master Builders (FMB)★ and other organisations mentioned in Chapter 3 will be able to provide you with a list of builders who specialise in or have a lot of experience of building extensions, perhaps of the type you require (such as kitchen or garage extensions).

If you are commissioning a two- or three-storey structure, it is important to make sure that the builder has some experience in this area.

Conversion into flats

Converting a house into flats, or creating a 'granny flat' on one floor of a larger property, is a relatively straightforward operation. Finding a suitable partition point and dealing with the sound-proofing and fire regulations are the hardest parts, but it can be a much cleaner process than knocking flats back into a house. If you are lucky then a simple plasterboard partition will suffice, though there will inevitably be electrical work and plumbing issues to deal with.

Building Regulations

Comprehensive regulations are in place to ensure that fire and sound cannot travel freely between dwellings, also that there is suf-ficient access and ventilation, an escape route in the event of a fire, and drainage and waste-disposal facilities. Heating controls and insulation may need to be upgraded.

Creating separate kitchen and bathroom facilities creates red tape. Open-plan kitchen designs can be ideal for smaller spaces. The kitchen is a major fire hazard and on upper floors it must be sited away from the exit, so that people in other rooms fleeing, say, a blazing chip-pan fire do not have to pass it on their way out.

Planning permission

Usually this will be necessary, because splitting a building into flats involves a change of use from the original terms under which plan-ning permission was granted. It is always required if you are creating separate dwellings with independent kitchen and bathroom facilities. It may not be appropriate to apply for formal permission for a 'granny flat' if the occupant is sharing the main facilities of the house, but the planning department needs to be notified so it can decide.

The most common problems

- **Plumbing** If the new flats are to be self-contained, separate plumbing and heating will be required, and a means of accessing the soil stack needs to be considered.
- **Siting suitable bathroom facilities** If there is only one bathroom in the house you need to find a suitable room close to the soil stack and drainage pipes, and work outwards with your design from there.
- **Separating the services** The electricity supply needs to be entirely rethought, and separate meters arranged for gas, water and electricity.

The biggest problems: soundproofing

Many complaints in converted flats are about noise. Airborne noise and impact transmission of sound are two distinct problems with separate solutions, and both need to be addressed by law.

Soundproofing sometimes happily doubles as thermal insulation, but it is still labour-intensive and costly to install, as is fireproofing. Building Regulations are very specific about what is required and the materials to be used, so there is not much scope for manoeuvre.

Putting in a floating floor

Isolating a floor from the beams supporting the ceiling below prevents a lot of structural noise transmission and is known as a 'floating floor'. If there is ornate plasterwork on a ceiling you won't want to disturb that, so you may have to take up the floorboards above in order to access all the joists and cover them with a layer of non-combustible, sound-deadening material (it is the same process for fireproofing). A floating floor is a good solution, though it is expensive and you lose a bit of ceiling height.

The sequence of events

1. **Stripping out** may involve removing old wiring and plumbing as well as preparing the properties for new independent services.
2. **The first fix** sees the installation of the first round of services infrastructure (see Chapter 7 for more detail).
3. **Erection of partition walls**, to facilitate access within the site, can come relatively late in the job.
4. **The second fix** involves fitting socket outlets and finishing touches.

Timescale: eight months to one year.

The case for using a specialist

Making two (or more) dwellings where formerly there was only one is more than a matter of an arbitrary division with some plasterboard partitions. As well as the services to separate there are detailed Building Regulations regarding sound- and fireproofing, and attention is also needed to ensure that communal areas don't become 'dead' areas, which can happen quickly if the stairs and hallways have a dark, boxed-in feel. An architect, if you are using one (see page 47), should be sensitive to these issues. A builder who is experienced in creating flats from houses can also have a considerable impact on the final outcome.

Finding a conversion specialist

Conversions are very often carried out by general builders, and finding one who is used to doing this sort of work is generally a matter of asking around. The FMB* and other sources listed in Appendix I should be able to provide you with a list of suitably accomplished contractors, but be sure to ask about their precise experience in this field, and ask to see examples of their previous work, visiting the sites if possible. Be wary of someone who says that they have only just begun working in the area.

Undoing a house conversion

Converting a house which has been used for flats back into a single dwelling is seldom as straightforward as it may seem. Structural changes are likely to have been made, either during the original conversion or later, as the different flat dwellers tailored their space to suit their needs. And very often the design of the new house you are converting back to will be different from the design of the original building. So a simple reconversion might involve taking out a staircase, while knocking through some rooms on the ground floor and extending the kitchen into the garden, all at the same time. If you are lucky you may be able to live in one of the flats as work goes on in the other, but this is not always possible and can also be extremely stressful. Hiring rented accommodation for the duration of at least some of the work is expensive, but it also focuses the minds of everybody involved (not least you) that time is money.

Building Regulations

As with all major building work, many aspects are regulated, but if you are converting separate flats back into a single dwelling, the biggest headache is likely to be the heating. The house is likely to require a larger heating system than any of the flats already provide, although if one of the boilers is operating with spare capacity you may be lucky and be able simply to add more radiators or link the two systems together. But it is more likely you will have to install a new, larger boiler, which will require approval, and possibly a change in the fuel source, which is also regulated. Under the requirements of Part L of the Regulations, this may also mean updating the heating controls.

Certain systems can only be installed by qualified experts and the installation of a new flue or the siting of a new gas or oil tank will also need to meet the Regulations. A liquefied petroleum gas (LPG) tank will need planning permission. The house may have to meet energy conservation requirements.

The most common problems

- **Planning permission** stymies more dreams than anything else, as initial designs are often drawn up over-eagerly without expert consultation.
- **Building control** can also seem like a brick wall you bang your head against, as designs may be rejected on grounds that don't make sense to you. Often a specialist firm will already have close working relationships with experienced local structural engineers,

architects and planners, and so will be able to navigate these obstacles more effectively than a general builder.

- **Recombining separate services** is a messy process which most builders hate. If space allows, it can sometimes be an advantage to keep two boilers operational so that you have independent supplies. If one breaks down, then you can always retreat to the other part of the house until it is fixed. However, keeping separate electricity supplies means dealing with two sets of bills.
- **Encountering asbestos** (see box , opposite).

The biggest problem: obtaining approval

Design and planning can be the largest headache. Working out a compromise between what you want, what you need and what you can actually achieve within the parameters of the existing house and the constraints of the Building Regulations is no small task. Often the potential of a building is difficult to appreciate from within the boxed-in confines of a clumsy conversion.

The sequence of events

This is the same as for an extension (see page 128), with the added complication that the messy 'knocking-through' process generally takes place earlier in the job and usually affects a reasonably central part of the house, making the chaos a bit more difficult to escape from.

The case for using a specialist

Converting a house into flats is definitely simpler than doing the reverse. Dealing with two sets of everything, trying to disentangle them and see which bits can be salvaged and what needs to go can be a nightmare. Often it's best to take everything out and start again, but sometimes that is not possible. Very occasionally one of the heating systems can be extended to supply the whole property, particularly if it was the original boiler for the house; but it all depends on how old everything is.

Finding a specialist at undoing conversions

Restoring a house to a single dwelling from two or more flats is a sensitive procedure and it is advisable to employ someone who is attuned to the original features. One way of gauging a builder's experience in this field is by researching your local architectural salvage merchants and then asking prospective builders what they think of them. See www.salvoweb.com* for a list of these in your area.

Timescale: nine months to one year.

What to do if you uncover asbestos

When work is being done on older properties, you risk finding asbestos. Asbestos has been known for its fire-retardant properties since the time of the ancient Greeks (they wove reusable handkerchiefs from it, cleaned by burning, which were issued to patrons of theatres during productions of 'weepies'). However, during the 1970s it was discovered that it causes mesothelioma (a degenerative lung disease) and lung cancer. Asbestos fibres, when damaged, fracture lengthwise into extremely fine particles which are too small to be dealt with by the excretion system of your airways. Thus tiny fibres lodge in the lining of the lungs and other passages where they gradually (sometimes over the course of many years) provide the conditions which allow tumours to develop.

Today if asbestos is discovered on commercial properties, it has to be recorded in a log which must be referred to before major work is carried out and passed on to the new owner with the deeds when the building changes hands. It is not uncommon in domestic conversions – fire doors in particular were often made up to specification by adding asbestos. Although there is no legal obligation, owners of private properties should record the existence of any asbestos uncovered for future occupants.

The key to dealing with asbestos is to create as little dust as possible. The general rule is to leave it undisturbed, although you may be able to take it out by undoing a few screws, gently lifting the panel out, wrapping it in plastic and taking it to a designated disposal site. For entrenched asbestos such as that found in flues, you should call in a specialist, which may entail costs and delays. It's a good idea when dealing with asbestos to keep it wet – that way, asbestos dust (the dangerous part) will not fly about. If in any doubt, leave it to a specialist.

Chapter 9

Dealing with disputes

So the dust has settled, the work has stopped – and you are not happy. Sadly this can often be the case with building projects, partly because there are so many variables within any job, partly because people fall prey to cowboy builders, and partly because customers' expectations can be unrealistic.

If you have a written contract, as discussed in Chapter 2, you are in a much stronger position in the event of a disagreement. With formal contracts you must, however, take particular care to follow notification procedures if you are dissatisfied with a builder's work or you think he is in breach of contract. If you have appointed a contract administrator it is his job to mediate fairly between you and the other party, and you should not interfere with his duties.

The overriding aim in resolving disputes is to be seen to be acting reasonably. An over-aggressive stance without regard to contractual obligations may well prejudice your case.

Establish the basis for your complaint

Disputes can arise around misunderstandings, particularly when subjective opinion about things such as finishes counts for so much. At other times the reasons for the dissatisfaction will be clearer; but before launching into a full-scale conflict with the contractor, withholding payments and taking on legal advisers, it is usually best to consider all the other options first.

Before complaining, be clear about the following things:

- **Why are you dissatisfied?** Was it the way you were treated? With builders this could just be culture shock. Apart from being a 'rough-and-ready' industry, full of 'colourful' characters, the building process itself is invasive and possibly even shocking for someone who hasn't been through it before.

Nerves are on edge, boundaries are overstepped and patience is stretched to the limit and beyond. Take a weekend away from it all to decide whether the complaint is really worth pursuing, or whether it would be best to make a compromise for the sake of the smooth running of the job. If you live in an area where good builders are scarce, you may want to employ the same person again in the future.

- **What do you want to happen as a result of the complaint?** Do you want an apology, financial recompense, or do you want the service that you feel should have been provided in the first place? In terms of any legal claim, the law aims to put you in the position you would have been in had the contract not been breached. Ordinarily this will equate to the costs of remedial work. It is unusual for the courts to order someone to carry out work of this type – they would normally award what it would cost for another contractor to complete or rectify the work done to date. Depending on the specific circumstances of your case, you may or may not be able to claim damages for any inconvenience or distress caused.

Keep your cool

In the event of a dispute it helps to stay rational and to keep track of developments in a calm and methodical manner.

- **keep a record** Log phone calls and other conversations soon after the event, making a note of what was said by whom and when, particularly if any agreements were made. If the exchange is in writing, don't forget to make a copy of your side of the correspondence. A 20p photocopy of a handwritten note may mean the difference between having your claim upheld or dismissed
- **keep the evidence** Retain all receipts, invoices, letters and emails. Keep the originals safe and make photocopies.
- **keep calm** Confrontation produces adrenaline, which can lead to physical hostility, so take precautions against getting carried away by the moment. Before confronting someone, visualise the encounter and imagine yourself dealing with the person confidently. Have a plan of action so you know what to do when they arrive. Don't be afraid to use humour if appropriate,

but try not to threaten the person or make sarcastic remarks. It may help to say that you have taken appropriate advice and that you are prepared to resolve the matter amicably. Try to avoid falling out with your builder and letting a clash of personalities destroy an otherwise businesslike relationship.

Put it in writing

Any important courses of action – for example, warning that you will need to instruct someone else to complete the work, or threats of legal action – should always be put in writing. Keep your correspondence simple and to the point. Long, rambling letters tend to find their way to the bottom of the pile and colour the recipient's view of the complainant.

Confronting the builder

Trying to resolve things in a conversation is preferable to a formal letter in the very early stages of a dispute. If this does not work, write to the contractor under the terms for disputes outlined in the contract. Quote the relevant clauses and make it formal but not threatening. If the dispute can be solved by letter this is generally a good option for everybody. If this does not work, you may want to write a more formal letter setting out the breach of contract and its consequences – for example, stating that if the builder does not return to carry out remedial work, another contractor will be instructed to complete the work. If you do this, it is advisable to get several estimates and give the builder one final chance to change his mind before proceeding with another contractor.

Office of Fair Trading (OFT)★ guidelines also recommend the following.

- Do not withhold payment lightly, as there is nothing to stop him taking you to court to retrieve money owed to him (see 'Withhold payment for single defects only, not the entire job', page 142). However dissatisfied you are, it may be necessary to pay him and then claim the money back through the court.

This should be accompanied by a letter stating that payment is made under protest and reserving your legal rights.

- Find a balance between acknowledging the work that has been carried out, and the shortfall which you are unhappy about. You should give the builder a chance to make amends himself before pursuing other avenues, and pay him for work which has been done satisfactorily. If you can show that you have acted reasonably throughout, then you will be in a stronger position when it comes to awarding compensation.

- Take photographs to support other evidence such as letters and receipts.

- Write to the builder to make 'time of the essence of the contract', and setting a specific date after which you will consider him to be in breach of contract (see page 37). (The new deadline has to be reasonable – setting a deadline of the next day would in most cases be deemed unreasonable). After this date you are free to seek other firms to finish off the work, charging the original builder for the cost (depending on the terms of your contract). The contractor should be comparable, i.e. if you originally went for a budget conservatory company you could find it difficult to justify the cost of getting a top end firm to complete the work.

- Get an expert opinion on work carried out. You could put forward the names of experts (if possible two or three) who you propose to use, and try to get the builder to agree to one of them. Try to appoint an expert who is acceptable to the builder. This can save the costs of duplicating experts' fees, and may lead to an agreement. If the builder will not agree to an expert you choose, he may agree to an institution naming an expert. Make sure the expert has no connection with you or the builder, as you want someone who is completely independent. If the builder objects to any of the people you propose to use, ask him to put his objections in writing. You may want to demonstrate to the judge that the builder is being unreasonable in refusing any name you put forward.

If all these measures fail you should seek reimbursement of the costs from the original builder. If he refuses to pay you could consider taking court action (see 'Going to Court', page 147). If you take this step you must make sure that he has been warned and it may be necessary to follow the 'Protocol' set out in the Courts civil procedure rules (CPR). The Protocol for Construction and Engineering disputes requires the parties to define the dispute and attempt to resolve it amicably before going to court. The Protocol may be found on the Court Service website *www.dca.gov.uk*.

Know your rights

Although a detailed written contract will give you stronger safe-guards, the law offers a degree of protection to all consumers, with or without such a document. If you are contracting for services, the Supply of Goods and Services Act 1982 implies into every contract a requirement that the work be carried out:

- with reasonable care and skill
- within a reasonable time (you can agree a specific timeframe)
- for a reasonable charge (if no price has been agreed)
- using materials that are of a satisfactory quality.

Work always has to be carried out with reasonable care and skill, but the reasonable time and charge provisions apply only when there is no specific agreement as to how much is to be charged for a job or when it has to be completed by.

The Defective Premises Act 1972 also provides that in respect of any building works carried out on a dwelling, the builder is under a statutory obligation to ensure that the work is done in a workman-like manner or in a professional manner with proper materials, so that the building will be fit for habitation when completed. This is usually implied in law, and most Standard Form Contracts used by builders contain a term to this effect. The Act does not, however, extend to Scotland

Under most Standard Form Contracts, the obligation to carry out the work in a workmanlike manner is a stricter duty than to do the work with reasonable skill and care – and it is therefore perhaps easier to pursue a builder for breach of contract rather than a breach of duty.

You can report a trader to the Trading Standards Institute★. This is the umbrella body for the local Trading Standards offices, which trade under slightly different names. You can find your local one at *www.tradingstandards.gov.uk*.

Your local Trading Standards office may already have a trader under investigation, and will probably be interested to hear of additional complaints. It can apply pressure to get complaints resolved. In addition, it can take action if someone falsely claims to be a member of a trade organisation such as the Federation of Master Builders (FMB)*, and may work with the trade association concerned to stamp out this sort of misrepresentation.

Your Trading Standards office can also use 'Stop Now' orders against traders who break the law. Contacting them will help prevent other consumers suffering at the cowboys' hands.

Withhold payment for single defects, not the whole job

Withholding the entire final payment because you are dissatisfied with, for instance, the grouting in the bathroom, is unreasonable. In this instance you should pay for all the work which has been completed to your satisfaction and withhold only the money for the grouting (or possibly all of the tiling, depending on whether the unsatisfactory finish has any underlying structural causes).

To take a guess on what sum to withhold is risky as if you overestimate the amount, a claim brought by the builder might be successful if he can show that you still owe him some money (i.e. you withheld more than was reasonable). It is a good idea to obtain an opinion about the likely cost of the work from a surveyor, who will be able to act as an expert if required.

Next, give the builder the chance to complete the job properly. If the work was done so poorly that you have lost faith in his ability, you could use the money withheld to employ another tiler. This may seem inconvenient and cause a small delay, but it is a small price to pay to achieve a psychological sense of 'closure'. Closure is an appropriate term for the completion of the construction process, because once the physical building work is finished it opens up a whole new world of living in your newly modified home – without the builders.

Typical problems

All of the situations below are unfortunately common with building projects. You can protect yourself by having a proper contract
where possible and following the steps described in 'Confronting
the builder'.

Delays

The phrase 'How long is a piece of string?' could equally be
'How long is a building job?' Both are notoriously indeterminate.
Delays are very much the norm on a building job. However, your
contract should specify that, even in the event of the delays
agreed to be unforeseeable, the builder should be seen to be making 'diligent progress' towards completion. Including a clause
outlining the precise number of days' absence which will be tolerated before damages are incurred is something to consider, particularly for a major project. This will then apply if a delay seems
indeterminate and the contractor is regularly failing to appear on
site. The clause will provide a fixed level of damages (known as
liquidated damages) per week by way of compensation. One
problem with tough clauses in your contract is that good builders
are always booked up and might prefer to work for someone with
less strict contractual obligations. However, a brief discussion
with your builder will determine his attitude to such things as a
time penalty (liquidated damages) clause, and if he prefers not to
have to guarantee his attendance then you may be better off
employing someone who will.

Poor workmanship

Work has to be carried out in a workmanlike manner, using
materials of satisfactory quality. Therefore the standard is not
perfection. The quality of workmanship can be argued about
indefinitely, and cases made and embellished with rhetoric on
both sides, but the fact remains that good-quality workmanship
does not give rise to debate (as long as expectations are reasonable – i.e. not expecting perfection). A serious builder will want
to know exactly what you mean when you criticise his work on
these grounds. He will either endeavour to put it right, or

explain to you in detail why he thinks your view of poor workmanship is inappropriate.

If you have an architect or other professional acting for you as contract administrator, talk to him about your concerns and be guided by his judgement. It could be that minor defects are being tolerated to facilitate the smooth running of the job, and are all being properly noted on the contract administrator's snagging list (see box on page 103) to be rectified before completion.

If you have to make a judgement yourself, be careful not to be too heavy-handed. However, you should not tolerate:

- anything left unsafe
- excessive levels of dirt or untidiness
- gaps between joinery such as skirting and architraves
- poor finishes
- noisy plumbing
- wobbly appliances
- wonky worktops
- bathroom furniture which is not level
- fixtures which are poorly secured (but wait until the end of the job before questioning these, as their situation may be temporary).

In general, these sorts of things can be referred back to the Schedule of Works (see page 43); but if you are genuinely dissatisfied and the contractor refuses to act, you should invoke the terms of your contract and withhold payment for that portion of the work when it is considered to be complete after giving the appropriate written notice.

Even if there is nothing in your contract about poor workmanship, or you don't have a contract, you can still withhold a sum equivalent to the cost of remedial work. Any such steps should be taken through the contract administrator, if you have one.

The contractor goes bust

Unless you have an Insurance Backed Guarantee (IBG – see page 44) or have paid a deposit by credit card (see box below) there will be no way of getting your money back.

> ## Let your credit card take the strain
>
> If you have the opportunity of putting any amount of payment for building work on a credit card then you should take it. As long as the value of the contract is between £100 and £30,000 and the amount put on the card is less than £25,000, then the card issuer is jointly and severally liable for any breaches of contract or misrepresentations that can be established against the builders. You don't have to have paid for all the work on the card – even a nominal deposit would make the card company liable to the full extent of any breach of contract/misrepresentation under Section 75 of the Consumer Credit Act 1974. This protection does not apply to payments made on debit and charge cards.

If there are unpaid subcontractors, don't be tempted to pay them off yourself, as your contract should state that their wages are the responsibility of the main contractor – who will probably owe you money as well because he is in breach of contract. Even if there is nothing in the contract on this point or you have no written contract, if you only agreed to pay the builder for the work done and he has subcontracted certain responsibilities to others, then he is responsible for paying them. The position would be different if you agreed to pay the subcontractors direct.

You may be able to keep any tools and materials which have been left on site, provided that these actually belong to the builder and have not been hired, but often the subcontractors will have sensed the impending financial disaster (as they will not have been paid) and they may have already had a free-for-all with any tools belonging to the contractor that are not nailed down.

Overcharging

Where nothing specific is agreed, a builder is entitled to charge a reasonable sum for the work done. It may be possible to determine what is reasonable by obtaining quotes from other local contractors to establish what the local market rate for the work is. You would in practice need as many quotes as possible – probably not less than three.

If it does not appear on the original schedule, extra work should have a price agreed in writing and be added to the 'extras' list before it is carried out. A quantity surveyor or architect would be able to advise on the cost of extras. Make it clear that this extra work doesn't alter any other aspect of the original contract and that the price for the work originally agreed remains unchanged. If no price is agreed for the extra work, then, as stated above, the builder is entitled to charge a reasonable price.

Dispute resolution

Arbitration

Most commercial-sector building contracts contain dispute clauses (although these are not mandatory) whereby disputing parties may choose to arbitrate rather than litigate, and will agree to be bound by the decision of an arbitrator who is independent and has no interest in the outcome of the case. There is some scope for appeal.

In the event of a disagreement, in a large-scale domestic job it can be a good idea to employ an arbitrator, who will reach a decision quickly (often within a month). A simple, objective assessment provided by an arbitrator can free up a badly log-jammed job.

Independent arbitrators may be professional arbitrators, surveyors, architects or lawyers working as arbitrators for the building industry. The Royal Institute of British Architects (RIBA)★ and the Royal Institution of Chartered Surveyors (RICS)★ offer arbitration schemes to non-members, as does the Law Society★ and the Chartered Institute of Arbitrators★.

In recent years there has been a tendency towards other forms of dispute resolution, such as mediation or conciliation, which may cost less and save time depending on the type of dispute. The terms are generally used interchangeably.

Conciliation is used as a more informal alternative to arbitration in some Standard Form Contracts. Mediation is a process whereby the parties resolve their differences through an intermediary called a mediator. It is voluntary, non-binding and without prejudice. In mediation, a specially trained third party will intervene in a dispute and attempt through negotiation techniques to bring the parties together in a settlement agreement. If the parties cannot agree, the dispute may be referred to arbitration or litigation.

Trade associations

Most trade associations have reasonably effective complaints procedures (see Appendix I), and often the mere mention of resorting to these will produce the desired effect. Builders who are trade-association members tend to value their membership, which provides them with many benefits, and are unlikely to want to jeopardise their relationship with the parent association. Although most redress mechanisms are quick and fair, some are cumbersome and procedures are occasionally weighted in favour of the trade-association member.

You should ask detailed questions about the nature of the association's complaints procedure. A good association will explain how this works (the Federation of Master Builders (FMB)★ and National Federation of Roofing Contractors(NFRC)★ give details on their websites). Find out about the likely timescale, and ask for a ballpark assessment of whether the outcome will be in your favour. Many respectable associations, such as the Confederation of Roofing Contractors★, operate according to the maxim that '99 per cent of the time the customer is right', so the onus may well be on the member to capitulate and put things right.

www.howtocomplain.com is an excellent website dedicated to the craft of effective complaining, with information and links explaining procedures and rights. *160 Letters that Get Results* (from Which? Books★) contains a chapter on building work, with relevant sample letters.

Going to court

This is the final sanction, not to be undertaken lightly as the consequences can be very serious for both sides. If the builder has insurance and/or the backing of a trade association, he will have his legal expenses covered and may be less troubled by the whole procedure than you are.

The County Court

The small claims court

If your claim is for less than £5,000 in damages in England (£750 in Scotland, £2,000 in Northern Ireland) and your contract has no dispute clause, then you may want to proceed to the small claims track of the county court (for claims above this amount, see 'Fast track and Multi Track', below). Pick up a claim form from the court and return it completed with the fee (the fees change from time to time and are on a sliding scale depending on the value of your claim. Consult a solicitor, or Citizens Advice Bureau (CAB)★, if you need assistance with filling in the form. You cannot recover any fees a solicitor charges you.

The form asks you to state your case and needs to be presented in triplicate so that there is a copy for you, the court and the builder. If you have included a credit provider, there will need to be another set. The court will send a copy of your form to the builder, along with a form for outlining his defence. Once the builder has filed a defence, an allocation questionnaire has to be completed. The court will then issue 'directions' which are steps the parties have to take such as disclosing documents they are each going to rely on, including expert evidence and reports. The court may ask for witness statements as well. A date for the hearing will be set, which will be presided over by a district judge.

Prepare your case thoroughly so that you can present it confidently – look at the defence and consider ways in which you can challenge what is going to be said in court. You may want to consult a solicitor or CAB for advice (as before, you probably won't be able to recover the cost of any solicitor's fees).

If you win your claim, the court fee is claimable from the opponent, as are certain other limited costs, such as fixed amounts for reasonable travel expenses and any loss of earnings for the day you have to attend the court (this is currently capped at £50). However, it can be a good idea to check that your opponent is likely to be in a position to pay up before embarking on litigation (see the advice in 'Fast track and Multi Track, below).

It is possible to navigate the small claims procedures without a legal adviser. Guidance from a legal advice centre, Citizens Advice Bureau (CAB) or Which? Legal Service★ (fee payable) can be valuable as these organisations can help you to present your case appropriately and recommend what sort of evidence to produce. You can find online advice on the small claims court procedure at the CAB website *www.nacab.co.uk*

Using the small claims court can be quite time-consuming: two to six months can elapse between submitting your form and the date of the hearing. A decision in your favour is satisfying, but you will not necessarily receive the compensation ordered by the judge straight away. If the opponent builder refuses to pay, you can return to the court, as there are a number of ways to enforce the judgement (see below). It will be your responsibility to choose one and initiate it.

If you lose the case, the defendant can claim back the same items of expenditure as you could if you won, although if they simply defend the claim they won't incur a court fee, so there would be no fee to claim back. If for whatever reason they have included a counterclaim, which has been successful, then the fee they will have paid to bring this will be recoverable.

Fast track and multi track

For amounts in excess of £5,000 but under £50,000 you will need to apply to the Fast or Multi track of the county court. Fast Track deals with claims up to £15,000, and the Multi Track with claims of £15,000 to £50,000. Legal representation is advisable. Before you consult a lawyer, it is a good idea to check whether the builder actually has money or assets for you to claim against. If he has no premises, equipment or insurance it will not be worth proceeding with your case.

Companies such as Callcredit★, Experian★ and Equifax★ charge a small fee for providing a credit reference; and a number of online credit-checking facilities can also provide information, although the amount of detail on small firms is limited. You could start by inspecting the builder's premises (if he has any) to see what sort of state they are in. If he has valuable equipment such as a new van or a JCB standing around, then it could be worth proceeding. Bear in mind that if the builder has the van or equipment on hire purchase, it can't be seized. To get him to pay up you can use the measures outlined in 'Enforcing judgement', below.

As with small claims you are required to complete a claim form, and in addition must file a statement of case. Your statement of case simply sets out the facts forming the basis of your claim and describes the nature of the dispute. It will refer to the terms of the contract, the Schedule of Works and, if relevant, include invoices, certificates and instructions. Documents referred to in the statement must be copied and attached for reference.

After the defence plea, the court will require the parties to complete an allocation questionnaire and later attend so the judge can give directions as to the conduct of the proceedings. The defendant must serve a defence, and the parties have to exchange lists of documents and evidence they intend to rely upon. They must also exchange expert reports and facilitate meetings of experts in an attempt to resolve technical questions. Following this, the court will fix a date for a hearing the parties can attend and present their respective cases. Legal professional advice is advisable, as is legal representation at the hearing.

The High Court

More complex cases over £50,000 may be heard in a specialist department of the High Court, known as the Technology and Construction Court (TCC). Judges here are experts in the construction field. The procedure is similar to that outlined above, although the TCC judge may give more specific instructions to suit the circumstances of the case. Special directions are often given with regard to the preparation of schedules and expert evidence, and the options described in 'Enforcing judgement' (below) apply. The court is renowned for its innovative procedures and its user-friendly approach. Again, it is important to take legal advice.

Enforcing judgement

The following methods can be used to extract payment if a builder refuses to meet the compensation demanded by a court.

- A **third party debt order** can be served on a third party who owes or is holding money for the builder (such as his bank), instructing them to pay money to you instead. The third party can object at a hearing.
- An **attachment of earnings** order will allow you to deduct

money from the builder's earnings directly, though not if he is self-employed.

- You can apply for an **oral examination** which requests the opponent to come to court to be questioned by a judge, though he does not have to answer. If he refuses you can apply to the court for an order to force him to do so, after which he will be in contempt of court. Ultimately the penalty for this is imprisonment.
- A **warrant of execution** authorises bailiffs to enter property and seize goods of sufficient value at auction to pay a judgement fee plus the costs and fees incurred in extracting the goods. This is a fairly extreme measure and is best reserved as a last-resort option.
- You can petition to make the builder **bankrupt** if the amount owed is over £750 and you have already issued a statutory demand or tried to collect the money using the bailiffs. If a court hearing sanctions the bankruptcy, a trustee will try to recover as much creditors' money as possible.
- If the builder works for a limited company, then you could petition to **wind up** the company (although you should bear in mind there may be other creditors ahead of you in the pecking order. Will there be anything left for you?).

Before resorting to any of the measures above, you could try writing to the builder warning him of your intention to apply for a warrant of execution; if you have successfully navigated the small claims procedure and won against him, it should be easy to convince him that you will follow through with your threat.

Appendix I: Trade Associations

This directory lists some of the largest and best-known trade associations. It describes the composition of each body and what steps it takes to regulate the work of its members. For contact details see the addresses section at this back of the book. Details are correct at the time of going to press but you should check with each organisation directly in case of doubt.

General builders

The Federation of Master Builders

The Federation of Master Builders (FMB)★ is the largest body of general builders. The membership breaks down as follows:

- 85% carry out general building work
- 33% carry out new house building
- 34% carry out or specialise in roofing
- 22% carry out or specialise in industrial and commercial work
- 12% carry out or specialise in electrical work
- 16% carry out or specialise in flooring and tiling
- 12% carry out or specialise in heating/ventilation
- 7% specialise in civil engineering.

The FMB has over 75 trade categories. Fifty-one per cent of FMB members employ five people or fewer, and 13 per cent work on their own. Less than 10 per cent of members employ more than 30 staff. Eighty per cent of members say that the majority of their turnover comes from repair, maintenance and improvement work from the public and private sectors.

At the Internet site *www.findabuilder.co.uk*, users can access the FMB database of members. They type in the first part of their post-code, select the relevant trades and a list of up to 15 FMB local members is provided.

The FMB also provides advice to consumers, and offers con-tracts in Plain English which have been vetted by the Office of Fair Trading.

Membership 13,000.

Membership fee £312.

Membership requirements Members must have been trading for at least a year, provide at least six customer references (including one from a professional source), and demonstrate good financial health. Each applicant's business address and VAT status are checked, and local branch approval is required in order to join.

Distribution Mainland UK and Northern Ireland, including the Isle of Man, the Channel Islands, the Scottish Isles and the Isle of Wight.

Complaints procedure Each region has a complaints committee (half of whose members are independent of the FMB) which will endeavour to settle disputes amicably. If this is not possible, third-party intervention is offered. Ultimately the FMB can decide on a range of options, from dismissing the complaint to expelling the FMB member.

Insurance Members must carry all legally required employer's and public liability insurance. Members can pay an extra £135 to be able to offer a ten-year MasterBond warranty, which covers house extensions, loft conversions, refurbishments, central heating instal-lation, double-glazing work, wall insulation and other structural and decorative work. It costs the customer 1.5 per cent of the total project cost. It protects against defects due to faulty workmanship or materials for two years, and against structural defects for ten years. Should the builder be declared bankrupt while work is in progress, the warranty will provide either 25 per cent of the contract price or £10,000, whichever is the lesser, for another MasterBond builder to complete the contract.

Spot checks on members' work The FMB will investigate mem-bers only if complaints have been made against them.

Guild of Master Craftsmen

The objective of the Guild is to preserve high standards and promote the professional expertise of its members. It also provides marketing advice to members. Successful applicants receive a 'Certificate of Quality and Service'.

Firms may be granted approval to use the Guild's seal on their product or service after undergoing tests and an assessment by the Council of Management.

Membership Undisclosed. Includes Aston Martin and Jane Asher Party Cakes, as well as the odd general builder who will come round and fix your roof.

Membership fee Differs according to category of trade.

Membership requirements As well as demanding expertise in members' chosen areas, the Guild emphasises the words 'skill' and 'integrity'.

Distribution National.

Complaints procedure Conciliation is offered.

Insurance Members must carry all legally required employer's and public liability insurance. No bankruptcy cover is given through the Guild while work is continuing: insurance is recommended.

Spot checks on members' work The Guild will investigate members only if complaints have been made against them.

Homepro

Homepro★ was formed in 1999 to provide a mainly Internet-based directory of reliable building firms. It has since expanded to absorb Fairtrades, a similar organisation founded 18 years ago which still trades under its own name. Homepro can provide a standard Building Works Contract.

Membership 5,000+.

Membership fee £175.

Membership requirements Members must have been trading for a minimum of one year, have a clean legal history and be in excellent financial health. They must also have ten randomly selected customer job files verified independently (seven of which must provide positive feedback), and must agree to abide by the Homeowner Charter, designed to make your home improvement projects less stressful. The Charter includes a commitment to: supply a written quotation; comply with all laws and building regulations; maintain adequate insurance; respect customers' privacy, security and safety; work tidily and have good timekeeping.

Distribution National.

Complaints procedure Conciliation service available.

Insurance Homepro members can offer their own Insurance Backed Guarantee (IBG). The IBG covers repayment of your deposit should the company cease to trade, any additional costs of completing unfinished work with an alternative contractor, and rectification of defects in the work. Work is guaranteed for up to ten years.

Spot checks on members' work Companies are given scores when they are first assessed for membership; these scores are updated constantly whenever a contract is completed. They are visible on the website at *www.homepro.com*.

League of Professional Craftsmen

The League of Professional Craftsmen★ was formed to represent businesses that use a high degree of skill or expertise in their everyday work, and to counteract the prevalence of tradesmen producing poor-quality work who claim to be craftsmen.

The League guarantees that its members will complete a professional job, on time and for an agreed price. Members have permission to display the League's logo on their letterhead and advertising material in order to reassure customers of their credentials.

Membership Approx 3,000.

Membership fee Up to £588.

Membership requirements Applicants must provide references from three customers giving feedback on how the work was completed. After membership is granted, the League issues a Letter of Quality Assurance that members can pass on to customers, which includes a Mediation Contract in case of dispute.

Distribution National.

Complaints procedure A mediation service and informal complaints procedure are available.

Insurance Members must carry all legally required employer's and public liability insurance. The League recommends that an IBG be taken out, and will facilitate this, but does not offer its own scheme.

Spot checks on members' work Contractors are not routinely assessed after the initial membership vetting.

The Quality Mark Scheme

The Quality Mark★ scheme is an attempt by the Department of Trade and Industry to saddle up a posse and, in its own words, 'ride those cowboy builders out of town, once and for all. The scheme, which was piloted very successfully in Birmingham and Somerset, is now being adopted nationally, although coverage is still limited to 10 main areas including Leeds, Nottingham, Derby, east Kent and parts of Oxfordshire. However, many Quality Mark-registered firms say that they are prepared to travel long distances for work, so even if you live outside the designated area it is still worthwhile contacting the scheme.

Membership 400 at the time of writing (with 620 awaiting accreditation).

Membership fee Tradesmen with a turnover of less than £1 million sign up free.

Membership requirements Members must be technically competent, with appropriate levels of skilled staff. They must obey health and safety rules and display good management practices. They must also pass a financial health check and follow a code of practice governing relations with customers which covers quotes and contracts.

Distribution Pilot schemes are projected nationally.

Complaints procedure The complaints system is linked to the warranty scheme offered by all members (see below).

Insurance Members must carry all legally required employer's and public liability insurance. Tradesmen provide a warranty on all work as part of the quotation before starting the job. This provides financial protection for up to six years against insolvency, poor workmanship and major defects.

Spot checks on members' work Every member firm is visited annually, and investigations follow complaints.

Women-only firms

Women and Manual Trades (WAMT)★ was formed in 1975 to promote the welfare of women working in the building trade. It is *not* a registration scheme for vetting the work of its members, but exists to provide support, information and advice to women in the construction industry and to improve conditions of training and employment.

As all of its members are female, WAMT offers a choice to those who like to use women contractors (this might be the preference of women who are alone in the house, for example). WAMT regularly receives testimonials comparing the work and overall attitude of its members favourably against their male counterparts. WAMT has a directory listing self-employed tradeswomen in London and south-east England, but other members are spread nationally. They include plumbers, carpenters and joiners, electricians, painters and decorators, and general builders.

The organisation will not give out the names of its members, but you can obtain a copy of the directory by sending a cheque for £5.

Membership 600.
Membership fee None.
Membership requirements Members should be women working or training in the construction industry.
Distribution Mostly London and the south-east of England.
Complaints procedure No formal procedure has been found to be necessary.
Insurance All members carry public liability insurance.
Spot checks on members' work None.

Painting and decorating

Painting and Decorating Association

The Painting and Decorating Association* was formed by the merger of the British Association of Decorators and the Painting and Decorating Federation. Members range from the largest national painting contractors to small family businesses.

The Association seeks to uphold the professional status of its members and the painting and decorating industry, requiring members to comply with a Code of Practice and meet high standards of craft competency. It also provides advice on training and employment.

Membership Approx. 2,000
Membership fee Ranges from £130 for single operators up to £1,410 for the largest firms.

Membership requirements Members must have been trading for at least a year, have at least three references checked, and be financially vetted.

Distribution National.

Complaints procedure The arbitration service will hear both parties' cases; if matters cannot be settled amicably two independent arbitrators from outside the area will be sent to inspect the work. Shoddy workmanship will be put right at no cost.

Insurance All members must carry public liability insurance.

Spot checks on members' work At the time of writing, available in some regions such as Coventry, Preston and Gloucestershire; it is intended to extend this to national coverage.

Dulux Decorator Service

The Dulux Decorator Service★ is a registration scheme run by Dulux Trade paints to provide quality workmanship by trained professionals. Decorators can advise on colour matching and must produce a fully inclusive quote. They are obliged to comply with all relevant regulations, such as those laid down by the Health & Safety Executive.

Membership 1,300.

Membership fee From £200.

Membership requirements Applicants provide three references, and are quality assessed on the site of the job they are working on at the time of application. They are judged on technical competence, overall presentation, timekeeping, how they interact with the client, and tidiness. They must use Dulux Trade paints.

Distribution National.

Complaints procedure If a complaint is made, a customer service team will inspect the work. If the customer does not want the same decorator to return to make good, another member will be assigned.

Insurance All members must carry public liability insurance of at least £2 million. After the work is complete, customers must fill in a form to obtain a guarantee of one year. The guarantee is only valid if Dulux Trade materials have been used.

Spot checks on members' work Spot checks are made if there has been negative feedback.

Roofing contractors

There are approximately 39,000 roofing contractors working in the UK. The memberships of the two bodies below represent just over 1,000 of them. It is worth bearing in mind that 34 per cent of the Federation of Master Builders membership (approximately 4,000) also specialise in, or are equipped to carry out, roofing work (see page 00).

Confederation of Roofing Contractors

The Confederation of Roofing Contractors (CORC)★ claims that '99 per cent of the time the customer is right'.

Membership 540.
Membership fee £276.
Membership requirements Applicants are assessed on four examples of their previous work, selected at random and visited by the Confederation, plus a credit check and trade references.
Distribution National.
Complaints procedure If a written complaint is made, the contractor will return to address the problem. Failure to do so within 14 days may mean that membership is revoked. CORC will also advise members of the public on how to sue a roofer and navigate the small claims court procedures.
Insurance All members carry employer's and public liability insurance. Members' work is guaranteed for ten years.
Spot checks on members' work None.

National Federation of Roofing Contractors

Among the swathes of unregulated roofing contractors, the National Federation of Roofing Contractors★ (NFRC) aims to promote the interests of its members by ensuring that they provide a good service to the public.

The NFRC offers a technical advisory service to members and customers, and cooperates closely on training and recruitment matters with the Construction Industry Training Board★.

Membership 783
Membership fee Up to £1,500, according to the size of company.

Membership requirements Membership processing takes around three months, as at least three references are checked, and financial and legal inspections are carried out. Members must have been trading for a minimum of one year.

Distribution National.

Complaints procedure There is a formal procedure linked to the organisation's Code of Practice. Disputes and arbitration go through various regional secretaries who act as area managers, and the NFRC claims that in 99 per cent of cases disputes are resolved amicably.

Insurance Members must carry all legally required employer's and public liability insurance.

Spot checks on members' work Every year to 18 months, without prior notice.

Heating and ventilation engineers

CORGI

The Council for Registered Gas Installers* (CORGI) has a stranglehold on gas fitting. Any appliance connected to the gas supply must, by law, be fitted by a 'competent person' – which, in practice, means a CORGI-registered installer.

Operatives may be registered to carry out different types of work (for example cookers, central heating or pipework). Your installer's identity card should have a list of boxes with ticks against each item he is qualified to install, inspect or maintain. Non-registered installers working in contravention of Health and Safety Executive guidelines risk imprisonment.

Membership Approx. 44,000 gas installers employing 95,000 gas fitting operatives assessed for specific types of work.

Membership fee An initial fee of £371, then £176 per year.

Membership requirements Members must have core gas-safety qualifications.

Distribution National.

Complaints procedure CORGI will investigate complaints against members and non-members.

Insurance Registered firms usually carry public liability insurance of £1–2 million.

Spot checks on members' work Each year every registered installer is professionally audited by one of 150 inspectors, who will visit them at work to assess their technical competence and may ask to check other recent jobs.

Heating and Ventilating Contractors Association

Heating and ventilation engineers who belong to the Association do not always have to be CORGI-registered, unless they are installing gas appliances.

Membership 1,400.
Membership fee From £270, according to size of company.
Membership requirements Members must have been trading for at least two years and must undergo an Inspection and Assessment Scheme.
Distribution National.
Complaints procedure Well-established, with an arbitration procedure. Members risk expulsion if they are deemed to be seriously at fault.
Insurance Members offer a Double Guarantee scheme, and must carry public liability insurance of at least £1 million.
Spot checks on members' work Members are given a technical and non-technical audit every two years.

Plumbing

The Institute of Plumbing

The Institute of Plumbing (IoP)* was established in 1906 as an educational charity with the 'prime objective of improving the science, practice and engineering principles of plumbing in the public interest'.

The IoP lobbies the government for the compulsory registration of all plumbers and also acts as Secretariat to the World Plumbing Council, which exists to further the cause of the plumbing industry worldwide.

Membership 11,000.
Membership fee £52.
Membership requirements Members agree to abide by a five-point code, which includes a commitment to: perform competently; safeguard the environment and public health and safety; comply

with all relevant laws and regulations; broaden skills, knowledge and personal qualities; and uphold the dignity, standing and reputation of the Institute and of the plumbing and mechanical engineering services industry.

Distribution National.

Complaints procedure A form is issued with the member's name printed on it, which can be filled out by the customer and then returned to the Institute. Arbitration is offered, and ultimately members can be expelled.

Insurance Most members carry all legally required employer's and public liability insurance cover (customers are recommended to check with individual firms).

Spot checks on members' work If a complaint is made, a committee consisting of professional standards inspectors (such as Trading Standards officers) will investigate. The plumber whose work is in question will be given the opportunity to put the problem right or send in someone else to do the work.

Association of Plumbers and Heating Contractors

In England and Wales, the Association of Plumbers and Heating Contractors★ (APHC) is a trade association established to protect the interests of plumbers, but it belongs to the school which believes that regulation and high standards of customer service are beneficial to the industry as a whole. Along with the Institute of Plumbing, the APHC lobbies for registration of all plumbers.

Membership 1,400.

Membership fee From £300.

Membership requirements Established plumbers and heating contractors must abide by a customer charter.

Distribution England and Wales.

Complaints procedure Members are encouraged to handle their own complaints, but if their system breaks down customers can use the APHC's own complaints handling procedure, which is administered independently by the Plumbing and Heating Licensing Authority★. An arbitration service is also available.

Insurance All work is guaranteed for two years, during which time the APHC takes responsibility for remedying any defects. Most members have £2 million public liability insurance.

Spot checks on members' work Members are assessed at the time they join, and then complete a yearly self-assessment form.

Scottish and Northern Ireland Plumbing Employers' Federation

The Scottish and Northern Ireland Plumbing Employers' Federation (SNIPEF) is the trade association for the plumbing and heating industry in Scotland and Northern Ireland. Members range from sole traders to large construction companies. Like its sister body the APHC, the Federation emphasises the importance of quality of work and reliability in its members, and insists that employees of members carry registration cards. All work undertaken by member firms must be carried out by qualified plumbers, and apprentices must work under qualified supervision.

Membership 820 firms.
Membership fee From £300.
Membership requirements Applicants must submit an accountant's financial integrity statement; six customer references are needed, and one completed job and two in progress must be inspected. The local Trading Standards office is contacted in case any adverse reports exist.
Distribution Scotland and Northern Ireland.
Complaints procedure An independent arbitration and conciliation service is offered; an inspector will be sent to determine what remedial or completion work needs to be done.
Insurance Members must carry public liability insurance of £2 million, and are encouraged to offer self-insured warranty schemes. The Federation also offers a free Guarantee of Work Scheme which ensures that work will be carried out to a satisfactory standard.
Spot checks on members' work Inspections are based on criteria similar to those of the Quality Mark scheme (see page 00). Ten per cent of members are inspected yearly; other inspections are generally undertaken following complaints.

Electricians

Electrical Contractors' Association

A trade body, the Electrical Contractors' Association (ECA)* exists to regulate its members and protect the public from poor and potentially dangerous work. The ECA lobbies the government for tighter controls on electrical contractors.

The ECA estimates approximately 130,000 electricians are working in the UK, though only 2,087 are registered with them.

Membership 2,087.

Membership fee From £565.

Membership requirements Members must have been trading for at least three years.

Distribution England, Wales and Northern Ireland.

Complaints procedure If work is found to be substandard, members may be reprimanded or struck off.

Insurance Members must have all legally required employer's insurance, and public liability insurance of at least £2 million. Members can offer an ECA warranty which guarantees that electrical work must meet relevant standards. Under the terms of the warranty, a consultant will inspect disputed work which may then be rectified by the original contractor or another ECA member. Disputes are referred to an arbitrator.

Spot checks on members' work Members are technically assessed every three years.

SELECT*

Founded as the Electrical Contractors' Association of Scotland, SELECT is the Scottish sister organisation of the Electrical Contractors' Association. It works in the interests of members and customers to promote safety, quality and technical excellence, and offers training, health and safety and management courses. A Code of Practice aims to ensure good relations between member firms and customers. Disciplinary action may be taken if a member firm does not comply with SELECT's constitution and rules.

Membership 570.

Membership fee £324 plus levy according to annual turnover of member company.

Membership requirements Applicants must undergo a financial health investigation and provide references from two previous clients and their bank manager; all electricians employed by the company must have appropriate trade qualifications and comply with membership criteria.

Distribution Scotland.

Complaints procedure If a member firm has failed to rectify a problem, resolution is offered and a SELECT inspector may assess the work. The job will then be completed by the firm in question, or another SELECT member if this is not possible.

Insurance Members must carry all legally required employer's and public liability insurance; SELECT also recommends a contract-backed guarantee scheme to cover the work for a year after completion.

Spot checks on members' work A rolling programme of checks assesses tools, equipment and work done over the last year.

National Inspection Council for Electrical Installation Contracting (NICEIC)

Known as NICEIC, the National Inspection Council for Electrical Installation Contracting* was established in 1957 as a non-profit-making, voluntary regulatory body to protect the electricity-using public from faulty or inadequate wiring (about 9,300 fires a year are reported as having an electrical source). It now inspects more than 30,000 installations a year.

NICEIC operates a register of assessed contractors who comply with the Council's rules. Approved contractors are required to issue a safety certificate for all electrical installation work to confirm that it meets British Safety Standards.

Membership 10,300.

Membership fee £376.

Membership requirements Members must have been trading for at least six months, be suitably qualified, and have appropriate premises and equipment to carry out electrical work. They must also provide a written Health & Safety certificate and undergo NICEIC inspection.

Distribution National.

Complaints procedure NICEIC will send an engineer to examine any unsatisfactory work and, if the complaint is upheld, they will either encourage their member to put it right, or remedy it themselves under the NICEIC Guarantee of Standards scheme.

Insurance All contractors must carry employer's and public liability insurance of at least £2 million. An Insurance Backed Guarantee

(IBG) is available for work done, which does not cover the customer in the event of bankruptcy.

Spot checks on members' work Approved contractors are reassessed every year by one of 53 full-time engineering staff to check that they still meet NICEIC standards.

Addresses

Architects Registration Board
8 Weymouth Street
London W1W 5BU
Tel: 020-7580 5861
Email: info@arb.org.uk
Website: www.arb.org.uk

Association of British Insurers
51 Gresham Street
London EC2V 7HQ
Tel: 020-7600 3333
Email: info@abi.org.uk
Website: www.abi.org.uk

Association of Building Engineers
Lutyens House
Billing Brook Road
Weston Favell
Northampton NN3 8NW
Tel: (01604) 404121
Email: building.engineers@abe.org.uk
Website: www.abe.org.uk

Association of Consulting Engineers
Alliance House
12 Caxton Street
London SW1H 0QL
Tel: 020-7222 6557
Email: consult@acenet.co.uk
Website: www.acenet.co.uk

Association of Plumbers and Heating Contractors
Unit 14
Ensign House
Ensign Business Centre
Westwood Way
Coventry CV4 8JA
Tel: (0800) 542 6060
Email: enquiries@aphc.co.uk
Website: www.aphc.co.uk

Association for Project Management
150 West Wycombe Road
High Wycombe
Buckinghamshire HP12 3AE
Tel: (0845) 4581944
Email: services@apm.org.uk
Website: www.apm.org.uk

Brick Development Association
Woodside House
Winkfield
Windsor SL4 2DX
Tel: (01344) 885651
Email: brick@brick.org.uk
Website: www.brick.org.uk

British Gas
House Contact Centre
PO Box 50
Leeds LS1 1LE
Tel: (0845) 600 5001
Email: house@house.co.uk
Website: www.house.co.uk

British Property Federation
7th Floor
1 Warwick Row
London SW1E 5ER
Tel: 020-7828 0111
Email: info@bpf.org.uk
Website: bpf.propertymall.com

British Wood Preserving and Damp proofing Association (BWPDA)
1 Gleneagles House
Vernon Gate
Derby DE1 1UP
Tel: (01332) 225100
Email: info@bwpda.co.uk
Website: www.bwpda.co.uk

British Woodworking Federation
56–64 Leonard Street
London EC2A 4JX
Tel: 020-7608 5050
Email: bwf@bwf.org.uk
Website: www.bwf.org.uk

The Building Centre
26 Store Street
London WC1E 7BT
Tel: 020-7692 4000
Website: www.buildingcentre.co.uk

Building Guarantee Scheme (UK) Ltd
Construction Employers Federation
143 Malone Road
Belfast BT9 6SU
Tel: 028-9087 7148
Email: mbrowne@cefni.co.uk
Website: www.cefni.co.uk

Callcredit plc
One Park Lane
Leeds
West Yorkshire LS3 1EP
Tel: (0870) 060 1414
Email: info@callcredit.plc.uk
Website: www.callcredit.plc.uk

Chartered Institute of Arbitrators
International Arbitration Centre
12 Bloomsbury Square
London WC1A 2LP
Tel: 020-7421 7444
Email: info@arbitrators.org
Website: www.arbitrators.org

Chartered Institute of Building
Englemere
Kings Ride
Ascot
Berkshire SL5 7TB
Tel: (01344) 630700
Website: www.ciob.org.uk

Chartered Institute of Building Service Engineers (CIBSE)
222 Balham High Road
London SW12 9BS
Tel: 020-8675 5211
Email: enquiries@cibse.org
Website: www.cibse.org

Citizens Advice Bureaux (CAB)
Look in *The Phone Book* under 'Citizens Advice Bureaux'
Websites: www.nacab.org.uk
www.adviceguide.org.uk

Confederation of Roofing Contractors
72 Church Road
Brightlingsea
Colchester
Essex CO7 0JF
Tel: (01206) 306600
Email: enquiries@corc.co.uk
Website: www.corc.co.uk

Conservatory Association
44–48 Borough High Street
London SE1 1XB
Tel: 020-7207 5873

Construction Confederation
56–64 Leonard Street
London EC2A 4JX
Tel: 020-7608 5000
Email: enquiries@thecc.org.uk
Website: www.constructionconfederation.co.uk

Construction Industry Training Board
Head Office
Bircham Newton
King's Lynn
Norfolk PE31 6RH
Tel: (01485) 577577
Email: Information.centre@cibt.co.uk
Website: www.citb.co.uk

Consumers' Association
2 Marylebone Road
London NW1 4DF
Tel: 020-7770 7000
Website: www.which.net

CORGI *(Council for Registered Gas Installers)*
1 Elmwood
Chineham Business Park
Crockford Lane
Basingstoke
Hants RG24 8WG
Tel: (0870) 401 2300 (Customer Services)
Email: enquiries@corgi-gas.com
Website: www.corgi-gas-safety.com

The Court Service
Southside
105 Victoria Street
London SW1E 6QT
Tel: 020-7210 2266 (Customer Service Unit)
Email: cust.ser.cs@gtnet.gov.uk
Website: www.courtservice.gov.uk

Department of Trade and Industry (DTI)
DTI Enquiry Unit
1 Victoria Street
London SW1H 0ET
Tel: 020-7215 5000
Website: www.dti.gov.uk

Dulux Decorator Service
ICI Paints
Wexham Road
Slough SL2 5DS
Tel: (0845) 769 7668 (Customer Services)
Website: www.duluxdecorator.co.uk

The Electrical Contractors' Association
ESCA House
34 Palace Court
London W2 4HY
Tel: 020-7313 4800
Email: electricalcontractors@eca.co.uk
Website: www.eca.co.uk

English Heritage
Customer Services Department
PO Box 569
Swindon SN2 2YP
Tel: (0870) 333 1181 (Customer Services)
Email: customers@english-heritage.org.uk
Website: www.english-heritage.org.uk

Equifax plc
Credit File Advice Centre
PO Box 1140
Bradford BD1 5US
Tel: (0870) 010 0583
Email: contactcis.uk@equifax.com
Website: www.equifax.co.uk

Experian Ltd
Consumer Help Service
PO Box 8000
Nottingham NG1 5GX
Tel: (0870) 241 6212
Email: experian_consumerhelp@experian-mail.custhelp.com
Website: www.experian.co.uk

Federation of Master Builders
Gordon Fisher House
14–15 Great James Street
London WC1N 3DP
Tel: 020-7242 7583
Email: central@fmb.org.uk
Website: www.findabuilder.co.uk

Glass and Glazing Federation
44–48 Borough High Street
London SE1 1XB
Tel: 020-7403 7177
Email: info@ggf.org.uk
Website: www.ggf.org.uk

Guarantee Protection Insurance Company Ltd
27 London Road
High Wycombe
Buckinghamshire HP11 1BW
Tel: (01494) 447049
Email: Shirley@gptprotection.co.uk
Website: www.gptprotection.co.uk

Guild of Master Craftsmen
166 High Street
Lewes BN7 1XU
Tel: (01273) 478449
Email: theguild@thegmcgroup.com
Website: www.guildmc.com

Health & Safety Executive (HSE)
HSE Infoline
Caerphilly Business Park
Caerphilly CF83 3GG
Tel: (08701) 545500
Email: hseinformationservices@nabrit.com
Website: www.hse.gov.uk

Heating and Ventilating Contractors' Association
ESCA House
34 Palace Court
London W2 4JG
Tel: 020-7313 4900
Email: contact@hvca.org.uk
Website: www.hvca.org.uk

HM Customs and Excise
Tel: (0845) 010 9000 (National Advice Service)
Website: www.hmce.gov.uk

Homepro
Quadrant House
The Quadrant
Hoylake
Wirral CH47 2EE
Tel: (08707) 344344
Email: info1@homepro.com
Website: www.homepro.com

Improveline
Bond House
347–353 Chiswick High Road
London W4 4HS
Tel: (0845) 359 3000
Email: info@improveline.com
Website: www.improveline.com

Independent Warranty Association
Spring House
1 Spring Gardens
Northampton NN1 1LX
Tel: (01604) 604511

Institute of Domestic Heating and Environmental Engineers
Dorchester House
Wimblestraw road
Berinsfield
Wallingford
Oxford OX10 7LZ
Tel: (01865) 343096
Email: info@idhe.org.uk
Website: www.idhe.org.uk

Institution of Electrical Engineers (IEE)
Savoy Place
London WC2R 0BL
Tel: 020-7240 1871
Email: postmaster@iee.org
Website: www.iee.org

Institute of Plumbing (IoP)
64 Station Lane
Hornchurch
Essex RM12 6NB
Tel: (01708) 472791
www.plumbers.org.uk

Institute of Quality Assurance
12 Grosvenor Crescent
London SW1X 7EE
Tel: 020-7245 6722
Email: iqa@iqa.org
Website: www.iqa.org

Institution of Structural Engineers
11 Upper Belgrave Street
London SW1X 8BH
Tel: 020-7235 4535
Email: mail@istructe.org.uk
Website: www.istructe.org.uk

Joint Contracts Tribunal (JCT)
9 Cavendish Place
London W1G 0QD
Tel: 020- 7637 8650
Email: stanform@jctltd.co.uk
Website: www.jctltd.co.uk

The Kitchen Bathroom Bedroom Specialists Association (KBSA)
12 Top Barn Business Centre
Holt Heath
Worcester WR6 6NH
Tel: (01905) 726066 (Customer Helpline)
Email: info@kbsa.co.uk
Website: www.kbsa.co.uk

The Law Society
The Law Society's Hall
113 Chancery Lane
London WC2A 1PL
Tel: 020-7242 1222
Email: info.services@lawsociety.org.uk
Website: www.lawsoc.org.uk

League of Professional Craftsmen
Suite 111
Marlborough House
159 High Street
Wealdstone
Middlesex HA3 5DX
Tel: 020-8427 8934
Email: Jacqui@confederation.co.uk
Website: www.buildingconservation.com

Loft Centre Products
Thicket Lane
Halnaker
Chichester PO18 0QS
Tel: (01243) 785 246
Email: sales@loft-centre-products.co.uk
Website: www.loft-centre-products.co.uk

The Loft Shop Ltd
Eldon Way
Littlehampton
West Sussex BN17 7HE
Tel: (0870) 604 0404
Email: enquiries@loftshop.co.uk
Website: www.loftshop.co.uk

National Association of Plumbing, Heating and Mechanical Services Contractors (NAPH&MSC)
Ensign House
Ensign Business Centre
Westwood Way
Coventry CV4 8JA
Tel: (01203) 470626

National Federation of Roofing Contractors (NFRC)
24 Weymouth St
London W1G 7LX
Tel: 020-7436 0387
Email: info@nfrc.co.uk
Website: www.nfrc.co.uk

National Inspection Council for Electrical Installation Contracting (NICEIC)
Vintage House
37 Albert Embankment
London SE1 7UJ
Tel: 020-7564 2323
Technical Helpline: 020-7564 2320
Website: www.niceic.org.uk

Office of the Deputy Prime Minister
Building Regulations Division
18/B Portland House
Stag Place
London SW1E 5LP
Tel: 020-7944 5742
Email: br@odpm.gsi.gov.uk
Website: www.odpm.gov.uk

Office of Fair Trading (OFT)
Fleetbank House
2–6 Salisbury Square
London EC4Y 8JX
Tel: 020-7211 8000
Email: enquiries@oft.gov.uk
Website: www.oft.gov.uk

Painting and Decorating Association
32 Coton Road
Nuneaton
Warwickshire CV11 5TW
Tel: 024-7635 3776
Website: www.
paintingdecoratingassociation.co.uk

The Quality Mark Scheme
PO Box 445
Tower Court
Foleshill Enterprise Park
Foleshill Road
Coventry CV6 5NX
Tel: (0845) 300 80 40 (Local rate)
Email: qualitymarkscheme@capita.co.uk
Website: www.qualitymark.org.uk

Quotecheckers
Website: www.quotecheckers.co.uk
Email: thegoodguys@quotecheckers.co.uk

Royal Incorporation of Architects in Scotland (RIAS)
15 Rutland Square
Edinburgh EH1 2BE
Tel: (0131) 229 7205
Email: info@rias.org.uk
Website: www.rias.org.uk

Royal Institute of British Architects (RIBA)
66 Portland Place
London W1B 1AD
Tel: 020-7307 3700
Website: www.architecture.com

Royal Institution of Chartered Surveyors (RICS)
12 Great George Street
Parliament Square
London SW1P 3AD
Tel: 020-7222 7000
Email: contactrics@rics.org
Website: www.rics.org.uk

Royal Society of Architects in Wales
Bute Building
King Edward VII Avenue
Cathays Park
Cardiff CF10 3NB
Tel: 029-2087 4753
Email: rsaw@instiriba.org
Website: www.architecture-wales.com

Royal Society of Ulster Architects
2 Mount Charles
Belfast BT7 1NZ
Tel: 028-9032 3760
Email: info@rsua.org.uk
Website: www.rsua.org.uk

Salvo
PO Box 333
Cornhill on Tweed
Northumberland TD12 4YJ
Tel: (01890) 820333
Email: admin@salvo.com
Website: www.salvoweb.com

Scottish and Northern Ireland Plumbing Employers' Federation (SNIPEF)
2 Walker Street
Edinburgh EH3 7LB
Tel: (0131) 225 2255
Email: info@snipef.org
Website: www.snipef.org

SELECT
The Walled Garden
Bush Estate
Midlothian EH26 0SB
Tel: (0131) 445 5577
Email: admin@select.org.uk
Website: www.select.org.uk

The Stationery Office
PO Box 29
Norwich NR3 1GN
Tel: (0870) 600 5522
Email: customer.services@tso.co.uk
Website: www.tso.co.uk

The Trading Standards Institute
4/5 Hadleigh Business Centre
351 London Road
Hadleigh
Essex SS7 2BT
Tel: (0870) 872 9000
Email: institute@tsi.org.uk
Website: www.tradingstandards.gov.uk

Trussloft Ltd
Bellwood farm
Harrogate Road
Littlethorpe
Ripon
North Yorkshire HG4 3AA
Tel: (0800) 195 3855
Email: information@trussloft.co.uk
Website: www.trussloft.co.uk

Water Regulations Advisory Scheme (WRAS)
Fern Close
Pen-Y-Fan Industrial Estate
Oakdale
Gwent NP11 3EH
Tel: (01495) 248454
Email: info@wras.co.uk
Website: www.wras.co.uk

Which? Books
Freepost
PO Box 44
Hertford SG14 1SH
Tel: (0800) 252100
Website: www.which.net

Which? Legal Service
Castlemead
Gascoyne Way
Hertford X
SG14 1LH
Tel: (01992) 822828

Women and Manual Trades (WAMT)
52–54 Featherstone Street
London EC1Y 8RT
Tel: 020-7251 9192
Email: info@wamt.org
Website: www.wamt.org

Index